Fig. 6 UPPER DECK (E)

Fig. 7.
MIDDLE DECK (F)

BUILDING THE TITANIC

Launch
OF

White Star Royal Mail Triple-Screw Steamer

"TITANIC"

At BELFAST,

Wednesday, 31st May, 1911, at 12-15 p.m.

Admit Bearer.

BUILDING THE TITANIC

AN EPIC TALE OF THE CREATION OF HISTORY'S MOST FAMOUS OCEAN LINER

Rod Green

Reader's Digest

The Reader's Digest Association, Inc.
Pleasantville, New York/Montreal/London/Hong Kong/Sydney

A Reader's Digest Book

This edition published by
The Reader's Digest Association, Inc.,
by arrangement with Carlton Books Ltd

Text and Design copyright © Carlton Books Ltd 2005

FOR CARLTON BOOKS
Editorial Manager: Lorna Russell
Picture Research: Sarah Edwards
Art Director: Lucy Coley
Cover Design: Alison Tutton
Design: Simon Wilder
Production: Lisa Moore

FOR READER'S DIGEST
U.S. Project Editor: Marilyn J. Knowlton
Canadian Project Editor: Pamela Johnson
Project Designer: George McKeon
Executive Editor, Trade Publishing: Dolores York
President and Publisher, Books & Music: Harold Clarke

Library of Congress Cataloguing-in-Publication Data:
Green, Rod
Building the Titanic: an epic tale of the creation of history's most famous ocean liner/Rod Green.
p. cm
Includes index.
ISBN 0-7621-0689-1
1. Titanic (Steamship)--Design and construction. 2. Shipbuilding--Northern
Ireland−Belfast--History--20th century. I. Title

VM383. T57G74 2005
623.82'432--de22   2005044307

Address any comments about *Building the Titanic* to:
The Reader's Digest Association, Inc.
Adult Trade Publishing
Reader's Digest Road
Pleasantville, NY 10570-7000

For more Reader's Digest products and information, visit our website
www.rd.com (in the United States)
www.readersdigest.ca (in Canada)

Printed in Dubai
1 3 5 7 9 10 8 6 4 2

The publishers would like to thank the following sources for their kind permission to reproduce
the pictures in this book. The page numbers for each of the photographs are listed below,
giving the page on which they appear in the book and any location indicator (l-left, r-right).

Aquarius Collection: Rank: 149
Christies Images Ltd 1996: 14
Corbis Images: Bettmann: 132-133, 135, 142; /CORBIS SYGMA: 69; /Hulton-Deutsch Collection: 118-119; /Todd Gipstein: 83; /Ralph White: 110-11, 126-127; /Underwood & Underwood: 46, 68, 71
Fr Browne SJ Collection / Irish Picture Library: 60r, 63, 70, 72, 73, 78, 114, 121, 122, 123, 128, 132
Getty Images: Fox Photos: 30; /General Photographic Agency: 28, 140; /Henry Guttmann: 12; /J. A. Hampton: 24-25; /Hulton Archive: 8, 10, 19l, 20, 37l, 117, 134; /R. Lock/Fox Photos: 34-35; /London Express: 124; F. J. Mortimer: 80; /Miguel Riopa/AFP: 158; /Sean Sexton: 44; /Time Life Pictures/Mansell: 6, 79; /Topical Press Agency: 102, 131, 147; /Topical Press Agency/Hulton Archive: 106
Harland & Wolff Heavy Industries Ltd: 33, 37r, 39, 43, 50-51, 52, 53, 54- 55, 56-57, 59, 64, 65, 75, 82, 84-85, 86, 90, 91r, 95, 96-97, 98-99, 101, 105, 108-109, 144, 150, 150-151, 153, 155
Illustrated London News Picture Library: 16-17, 22-23
Mary Evans Picture Library: 11, 13, 19r, 27, 40-41, 66-67, 138-139
TopFoto.co.uk: 60l, 74, 76, 136, 138, 141
Harland & Wolff Collection at Ulster Folk & Transport Museum: 2, 58, 66, 88-89, 91, 92-93, 94, 120

Every effort has been made to acknowledge correctly and contact the source and/or copyright
holder of each picture and Carlton Books Limited apologizes for any unintentional errors
or omissions that will be corrected in future editions of this book.

CONTENTS

The *Titanic* arrived at Southampton in time to catch the midnight tide on April 3, 1912, and tied up at berth 44, where she would remain for the next week, flying flags to celebrate Easter and the people of the town, even though belowdecks the crew was struggling to extinguish a fire in one of No. 6 boiler room's bunkers that raged for her entire stay at the port.

INTRODUCTION

Ask anyone on the streets of a major city anywhere in the world—London, New York, Paris, Tokyo, Sydney—to name a famous ship, and the answer you are most likely to hear (providing you immediately discount the *Star Ship Enterprise*) is the *Titanic*. The multitude of books, films and TV specials about the sinking of the *Titanic* means that most of those people on the streets will be able to tell you that the world's most luxurious liner struck an iceberg and sank carrying some of the richest (and poorest) people ever to cross the Atlantic. They may even be able to tell you that the disaster happened during her maiden voyage. But ask them when it happened, and you will hear guesses of anywhere from the late-nineteenth century up to the beginning of the Second World War. I know—I've asked around. Not quite as far afield as New York and Tokyo, but enough people from enough places to realize that while people know the legend of the *Titanic's* short life, they don't really know the story of the *Titanic*. While so many know a little about her demise, relatively few know the story of the *Titanic's* birth in the Belfast shipyard of Harland & Wolff; yet the story of the building of the *Titanic* is integral to that of her tragic destruction.

The *Titanic* was launched in 1912, the year when, in America, William Taft was replaced by Woodrow Wilson as president, and Arizona and New Mexico became states, bringing the total number of states to 48. In Britain, Herbert Asquith was prime minister, and Captain Scott raced Amundsen to the South Pole. King George V was on the throne, speaking English with a pronounced German accent and retaining the family name of Saxe-Coburg-Gotha, despite ever worsening relationships between both Britain and Germany, and King George and his cousin the kaiser. While war was brewing in Europe, the situation in Ireland was also sliding inevitably toward armed conflict. The country was divided along religious and political lines, between Protestants and Catholics, Loyalists and Republicans. The *Titanic*, hailed as a modern-day marvel, was created in a country riven by strife that dated back centuries.

The *Titanic* could be described as a bridge between two different ages. She was the most modern ship afloat, with radio, electric lighting, elevators, a fully equipped gymnasium, a swimming pool—and the most up-to-date safety features, such as automatic watertight doors. Despite this, her basic construction involved as much brute force as it did finely calculated engineering. Welding was an art that had yet to catch on, so the *Titanic's* hull plates were held together with rivets that were hammered into place when red-hot, the plates overlapping like tiles on a house roof. She was built to a grand scale—the largest vessel afloat—but she was built using basic techniques that had changed very little since the construction of the first iron-hulled ships more than half a century earlier, even though the *Titanic* was ten times the size of those early ships. Furthermore, her up-to-date safety features were to prove woefully inadequate. The building of the *Titanic* taught the world fewer lessons than did her sinking.

Despite the shortcomings of her design and construction, none of which would have become apparent had she not struck the iceberg, the building of the *Titanic* was something of which the people of Belfast were, and still are, justifiably proud. The creation of the *Titanic* and her sister ship, the *Olympic,* was an immense achievement, showing that British ships were the most advanced in the world and that Belfast-built ships were the best. That the ship sank after hitting the iceberg (no other ship of the time would have survived such a trauma, either) could not detract from the quality of the craftsmanship that had gone into creating her sumptuous interiors. The luxury of the first-class fittings equaled the standard of the most expensive hotels in London or New York. A journalist from the *Southampton Times* and *Hampshire Express* who paid a visit to the *Titanic* in Southampton compared the *Titanic* with her sister ship, and noted: "One person said that the *Olympic* was all that could be desired, and the *Titanic* was something even beyond that!"

Why such luxury? Why such a size? Why was such a ship built at this time? The story of the *Titanic's* sinking is an enthralling tale, but the story of the building of the *Titanic* holds a fascination all its own.

New York's Ellis Island immigration facility opened in 1891 with the potential to process up to 7,000 new arrivals every day. In 1907, shortly after this photograph was taken, 1.25 million people entered America via Ellis Island.

CHAPTER ONE

WHY BUILD THE *TITANIC*?

When RMS *Titanic* set sail from Southampton on Wednesday, April 10,1912, she was not only the largest ship afloat; she was also officially the largest moving man-made object the world had ever seen. She was 882 ft. (269 m) long and weighed over 46,000 tons, so maneuvering the giant ship was a delicate business. Six powerful tugs were required to push, pull and generally shepherd her away from the quayside out into position in the River Test, where she could finally engage her engines to begin making headway under her own steam.

As she picked up speed in the narrow channel, the *Titanic* passed two other liners docked side-by-side at berths 38 and 39–the *Oceanic* and the *New York*. The *New York* was in the "outside" berth, closest to the *Titanic*. Built in 1888 on the Clyde River, the *New York* was one of the finest liners of her day, having won the prestigious Blue Riband award for the fastest crossing of the Atlantic in 1892, but she was no match for the *Titanic*. The new liner was more than 350 ft. (106 m) longer than the *New York* and over four times her tonnage, a difference in size that was to cause an immense problem as the *Titanic* powered past.

The surge of the *Titanic*'s wash created waves that flung the *New York* up and down with such violence that her six mooring lines snapped like threads. The *New York*, now floating free and unmanned, save for a handful of workmen, was then drawn toward the *Titanic*'s stern as helpless as a scrap of driftwood. A collision seemed inevitable, and the crowds that had gathered to cheer the *Titanic*'s departure (as well as many of those on the deck of the giant liner) could hardly believe their eyes. They had come to watch the greatest ship ever built depart on her maiden voyage; instead, it seemed as though they were about

to witness an embarrassing fiasco. The master of one of the *Titanic*'s tugs, Captain Gale of the *Vulcan*, managed to throw a line to the *New York*, but it, too, snapped. A second line was made fast by the workmen aboard the *New York*, and it held, allowing the *Vulcan* to bring the *New York* under control when she was just 4 ft. (1.2 m) from the *Titanic*. Disaster was narrowly averted, and the *Titanic* continued on her way to her first port of call at Cherbourg, France.

Given subsequent events, people could be forgiven for thinking that it might actually have been better for the *New York* to have made contact with the *Titanic*. A slow-speed collision would have caused relatively minor damage, but the *Titanic*'s departure would have been delayed while repairs were made, and she might not then have come to grief four days later in mid-Atlantic. While the collision between the *New York* and the *Titanic* was narrowly avoided, how had the situation come about in the first place? Shouldn't the pilot who was aboard the *Titanic*, directing her out of Southampton–as well as the

Right: The White Star Line became a major player in modern shipping with the launch of the *Oceanic* in 1870. Hailed as the world's first superliner, *Oceanic* was an innovative design, combining the hull and the superstructure rather than having the superstructure "bolted on" to the hull. She also had running water in every cabin.

Far right: The first scheduled transatlantic steamship passenger service was established in 1838 when Isambard Kingdom Brunel's *Great Western* took 14 days 12 hours to make the first of more than 70 Atlantic crossings.

Titanic's own officers and the harbor authorities—have foreseen the problem of the huge liner disturbing the *New York* and the *Oceanic* as she swept past? Perhaps this was because a similar situation had not arisen when the *Titanic* docked in Southampton six days earlier and the *New York* and *Oceanic* were tied up at berths 38 and 39 then, too. Part of the answer may lie in the fact that no one really had quite enough experience in dealing with a ship the size of the *Titanic*. The superliner was an entirely new phenomenon and, despite the fact that the *Olympic* was already operational, there was a great deal to learn about the handling of ships this big. *Titanic* did, after all, dwarf the *New York*, a ship that despite having been built 24 years earlier, still had 10 years of working life ahead of her. But if the *New York* was still capable of operating as a transatlantic liner, why did the *Titanic* have to be so much bigger? Why had she been built to such a grand scale? Why, indeed, had the *Titanic* ever been built at all? The answer involves money, profit, pride, prestige and international rivalry.

The Lure of the New World

On January 1, 1891, 15-year-old Annie Moore from County Cork in Ireland earned herself a shiny, new American $10 gold piece by becoming the first immigrant to pass through the Federal Bureau of Immigration's brand-new receiving station at Ellis Island, New York. Over 700 immigrants arrived that first day on the SS *Nevada*, SS *City of Paris* and SS *Victory* and Ellis Island was designed to receive up to 7,000 immigrants per day. New York was the main port of entry for the vast majority of immigrants searching for a new life in America, although ships carrying would-be Americans also sailed into Boston, Philadelphia, Baltimore, San Francisco, Savannah, Miami and New Orleans. Fleeing from poverty and starvation during the potato famine of 1845–50, Irish immigrants quickly became the largest single immigrant group in the United States.

But it wasn't just the Irish who were heading west. In the 1850s around 2.5 million people had traveled to America, almost a million of them coming from Germany and eastern

Europe, where they were leaving behind poor harvests, or political or religious persecution. After the end of the American Civil War in 1865, the number of immigrants heading for New York grew from a steady flow to an unstoppable flood. During the 1870s there were 11.5 million immigrants to America, boosting the U.S. population to 50 million and making New York the first state with more than 5 million inhabitants. This dramatic increase in the number of immigrants was not due solely to the ending of the Civil War. There was another factor that had a far greater influence than the end of the war. What affected the rate of immigration more than anything else was the coming of the age of steam.

In 1869 America's transcontinental railroad was completed when the Union Pacific and Central Pacific companies' tracks were linked at a ceremony at Promontory Point in Utah. Steam trains could now cross the country from coast to coast, cutting the New York to San Francisco journey time from three months to just eight days. America's vast hinterland was opening up in a way that had never been possible in the days of the wagon train, and settlers were being encouraged to move inland from the coasts with the lure of free land for farming out in the "prairie lands."

A number of important pieces of legislation, including the Homestead Act of 1862, had been introduced to galvanize the population of rural America. Under the Homestead Act, a settler over the age of 21 could stake a claim to a parcel of land of up to 160 acres (65 hectares). In this way, around 270 million acres (109 million hectares), roughly 10 percent of the United States, was handed over to small farmers. The railroad companies, with their ever expanding rail network, mounted poster campaigns and placed advertisements to market themselves as the ideal means of escaping to this emergent nirvana. But while they could certainly disperse the tide of immigrants efficiently cross-country, steam trains were not what delivered the new arrivals to America. Steamships were responsible for that.

The first crossing of the Atlantic by a steam-powered ship was in 1819 when the SS *Savannah* sailed from Georgia to Liverpool, taking 23 days. The *Savannah*'s voyage, however, did

Above: A Union Pacific Rail Road advertisement from 1869, the year in which lines from the East and West coasts met up in Utah to complete the transcontinental railroad. Passengers could now travel from New York to San Francisco in eight days instead of three months and could now reach the coast in "less than four days" from Midwest cities such as Omaha.

Opposite: While the White Star Line was keen to grab its fair share of the immigrant trade, there were huge profits to be made from carrying wealthier passengers who not only paid huge sums for luxury suites on board but also spent lavishly on fine wines and à la carte dining on board. This early advertising poster is clearly aimed at the more sophisticated traveler.

not immediately consign the fleets of transatlantic sailing ships to the breakers' yards, as her crossing was regarded as something of a novelty and she still used sails for part of the journey. The first scheduled transatlantic passenger service by steamship came in 1838 when Isambard Kingdom Brunel's *Great Western* crossed in 14 days 12 hours. The *Great Western* would go on to make more than 70 Atlantic crossings. But like the *Savannah*, she was a paddle steamer, and paddle

White Star Line

To UNITED STATES and CANADA

HOLIDAY TOURS

Walter Thomas

steamers were more at home in calmer river or coastal waters than in the storm-tossed Atlantic, where the rolling of the ship could lift the paddles—mounted on the sides of the ship—out of the water. Not only did the consequent noise and vibration give cause for concern among the passengers but, with no water to push against, the exposed paddle wheel would race faster and faster, a situation that could easily result in serious damage to the machinery.

A greater problem in the early days of the steamship, however, was the inefficiency of the engines. Steam engines used a huge amount of wood or coal—more than could sensibly be carried for a long journey. This problem was solved, in part, by Brunel, who would go on to prove his theory that steam-powered ships could be built bigger and carry more coal, when he launched the *Great Britain.* At 322 ft. (98 m) long, she was the largest vessel afloat—100 ft. (30 m) longer than any other ship. Bigger ships, along with huge improvements in the efficiency of steam engines, provided a tantalizing prospect for the owners of shipping lines.

The new steamships cut the Atlantic crossing from the five or six weeks taken by a sailing ship, to just 11 days when Samuel Cunard's *Britannia* made the journey in 1840. Steam-ships did not rely on the winds and could be expected to arrive in port at or around the scheduled time. They were also bigger and could carry far more passengers—the few dozen passengers on an average sailing ship became a few hundred on a steamship. By the time Brunel's *Great Britain* dispensed with paddles and became the first iron-hulled, screw-propeller-driven ship to cross the Atlantic in 1843, the future was clear. Steamships were going to become, bigger, better and faster.

By the early 1870s, more than 95 percent of the passengers arriving in New York disembarked from a steamship. Dozens of small steamship companies sprang up with, among others, the Hamburg-America Line, Holland-America Line, Leyland Line, Dominion Line, White Star Line, Red Star Line, Cunard Line and Inman Line all crisscrossing the Atlantic in competition with one another for freight and passengers. It seemed as though there was plenty of trade for all, with a massive increase in cargo from America—principally cotton, tobacco and wheat—and a

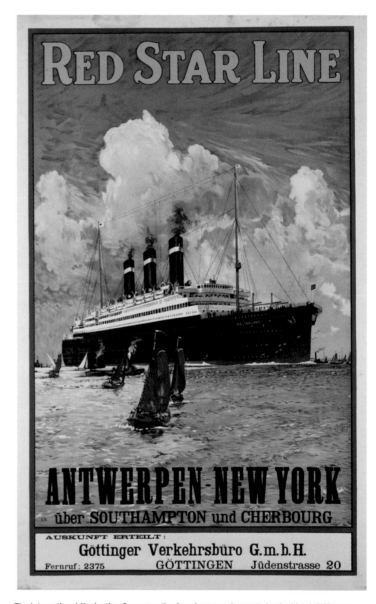

The International Navigation Company, the American conglomerate backed by J. P. Morgan that became the International Mercantile Marine Company in 1902, was perhaps better known as the Red Star Line. Although founded in Philadelphia in 1871, the Red Star Line was registered in Belgium under a subsidiary company and sailed to New York and Philadelphia via Southampton and Cherbourg from 1873. The Red Star Line finally disappeared when the company ceased trading in 1934.

blossoming trade in passenger traffic throughout the second half of the nineteenth century. The competition for business, however, coupled with a downturn in the American economy in 1873 that would be repeated again ten years later, and yet again ten years after that, meant that many of the new companies struggled to make a sufficient profit. Ships changed hands or were leased between companies, and amalgamations became inevitable, especially when American financier John Pierpont Morgan decided to take an interest in shipping.

Creating a conglomerate

J. P. Morgan's interest was inspired by two American ship-owners: Clement Griscom and Bernard Baker. Griscom owned the America Line and was also involved with the International Navigation Company of Philadelphia, which, in turn, had a major stake in the Red Star Line. Baker owned the Atlantic Transport Line (ATL), and in 1896 he also acquired the National Line operating out of Liverpool. Around the same time, Griscom took over the Inman Line of Liverpool. Both Griscom and Baker were keen to continue expanding their shipping interests. For Griscom, this meant seeking finance from the Philadelphia bankers Drexel & Co. (who had close links to the Morgan Bank in New York) to fund the building of six new ships. Baker, on the other hand, considered selling his Atlantic Transport Line to the British-owned Leyland Line, one of the biggest cargo shippers involved in the Atlantic routes. Griscom eventually persuaded Baker that the best way for them and the future of American merchant shipping to go was to pool their resources. Baker's ATL merged with Griscom's International Navigation Company, and the finance originally sought by Griscom now came from J. P. Morgan. The finance was not, however, simply for six new ships. In a surprising turn of events, the new conglomerate made some aggressive moves (generally attributed to J. P. Morgan), quickly acquiring the cargo-carrying Leyland Line, the Dominion Line and the prestigious White Star Line.

By 1902 the International Navigation Company, soon to change its name to the International Mercantile Marine Company (IMMC), was one of the most important shipping organizations operating in the North Atlantic. With J. P.

Morgan's help, Griscom and Baker, who had been the only American shipowners competing for transatlantic business, had created a force to be reckoned within the IMMC. Their ships sailed under the flags of three different nations: the United States, Belgium (the Red Star Line ships had been sailing from Antwerp to Philadelphia and New York since 1873 and were registered in Belgium under a subsidiary company) and Great Britain. The National Line, Inman, Leyland, Dominion and White Star lines were all British, operating British-built ships registered in the United Kingdom and flying the British flag.

The fact that so much American-owned shipping was in foreign hands was more than just an annoyance to J. P. Morgan. When competing for the contract to carry the U.S. Mail in 1891, the best and fastest ships of the International Navigation Company fleet were the Inman Line's *City of New York* and *City of Paris*. The government contract required that the U.S. mail be carried on ships capable of maintaining at least 20 knots on the Atlantic crossing between New York and Southampton. For carrying the mail, the U.S. government offered a subsidy grant of $8 per mile. The only drawback was that the *City of New York* and the *City of Paris* had to be reregistered as the *New York* and the *Paris* to sail under the American flag. The flag transfer was duly completed in 1892, but there were many who were unhappy about British assets being sold off to the Americans. By the time the IMMC bought the White Star Line in 1902, what was perceived as the gradual seepage of British merchant shipping into American hands caused an uproar in the British press. White Star's rival, the Cunard Line, was also in J. P. Morgan's sights, but the British government took swift steps to ensure that Cunard remained British.

Morgan's response was to step up the price war that the IMMC had instigated. He acquired a controlling interest in the Holland-America Line through a consortium formed with the major German lines, Hamburg-America and Norddeutscher-Lloyd. Morgan's aim in forming the consortium was not only to control prices on the transatlantic route but also to rationalize shipping schedules to ensure that New York, for example, did not see three different ships from three different lines all leaving for England on the same day. These three ships would have

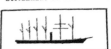

The First Cunarder, "Britannia" (1840)

This was one of the four vessels with which the Cunard line started : 207 ft. long, 1,154 tons, 740 h.p., speed 8½ knots ; took 12 days 10 hr. to cross the Atlantic in 1840

The diagrams give a striking impression of the growth of the transatlantic vessels which have brought England and America into such close touch. Starting from the "Savannah" of 100 ft. and 350 tons, which took 29½ days to cross over, we have reached the colossal "Mauretania," which is 787 ft. long and has a gross tonnage of 32,500, and will cross the Atlantic in less than a fifth of the time which was possible in 1819, when the "Savannah" essayed the task. Although the "Savannah" was the first steamship to cross the Atlantic she did not complete the voyage entirely under steam, her paddle-wheels being stowed on

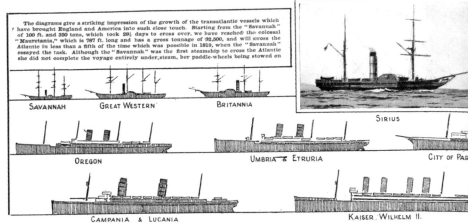

SAVANNAH   GREAT WESTERN   BRITANNIA

SIRIUS

OREGON   UMBRIA & ETRURIA   CITY OF PARIS

CAMPANIA & LUCANIA   KAISER WILHELM II.

		Length ft.	Gross Tonnage				Length ft.	Gross Tonnage
1819	SAVANNAH	100	350	1874	BRITANNIC		455	5,004
1837	GREAT WESTERN	212	1,340	1883	OREGON		500	7,375
1837	SIRIUS	178	703	1884	AMERICA		432	6,500
1840	BRITANNIA	207	1,154	1884	UMBRIA		501'6	7,718
1861	SCOTIA	366	3,870	1888	CITY OF PARIS		560	10,499

The White Star Liner, "Britannic" (1874)

Built in Belfast ; 455 ft. long, 5,004 tons, 5,000 h.p., speed 16 knots ; quickest passage 7½ days

The Guion Liner, "Oregon" (1883)

Built on the Clyde ; 500 ft. long, 7,375 tons, 7,375 h.p., speed 18·3 knots

H. B. Cull. '08.

The Turbine Cunarder, "Lusitania" (19

Built by Brown at Clydebank ; 787'6 ft. long, 32,500 tons, 65,000 h.p., speed 25 knots ; carries 500

The Cunard Liner, "Umbria" (1884)

Built on the Clyde ; 501'6 ft. long, 7,718 tons, 15,000 h.p., speed 20 knots ; carries 400 first, 200 second, and 500 third class passengers

The American Liner, "Philadelphia" (1888)

Built on the Clyde ; 527'6 ft. long, 10,499 tons, 20,000 h.p., speed 20½ knots ; carries 400 first and 250 second class passengers

The

Built at Belfast ; 565'8

Isambard Kingdom Brunel proved that steamships would operate more efficiently and more cost-effectively the bigger they became. This illustration shows how ship design changed and how quickly the steamships grew in size from the first ones to cross the Atlantic—the *Savannah*, *Great Western* and *Britannia* to the *Lusitania* and *Mauretania*.

uring the greater part of the run. The first ship which crossed entirely under steam was the l William," built at Quebec. The honour of beginning the great Atlantic ferry rests with the ," a small ship of 703 tons. She arrived at New York in 1838 after an eventful voyage a few ahead of a rival—the "Great Western." Shortly after leaving port the crew of the "Sirius" t to proceed in her, declaring it was unsafe to continue the voyage in so small a ship, and but energy and determination of her commander, backed by firearms, she would doubtless have put Eventually she arrived safely at her destination after a passage of about eighteen days

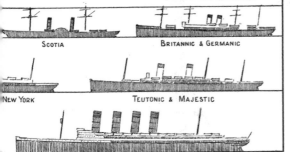

SCOTIA   BRITANNIC & GERMANIC

NEW YORK   TEUTONIC & MAJESTIC

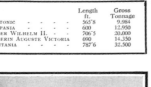

LUSITANIA & MAURETANIA

	Length ft.	Gross Tonnage
TEUTONIC	565'8	9,984
CAMPANIA	600	12,950
KAISER WILHELM II.	706'5	20,000
KAISERIN AUGUSTE VICTORIA	690	14,350
LUSITANIA	787'6	32,500

The Cunarder, "Scotia" (1861)

Built (of iron) on the Clyde; 366 ft. long, 3,870 tons, 4,200 h.p. She was described at the time as "the champion and model of a mercantile ocean steamship"

The Norddeutscher Lloyd, "Kaiser Wilhelm II." (1903)

Built at Stettin; 706'5 ft. long, 20,000 tons, 40,000 h.p., speed 23'58 knots; carries 775 first, 343 second, and 770 third class passengers

The Norddeutscher Lloyd, "Kaiser Wilhelm der Grosse" (1897)

Built at Stettin; 648'6 ft. long, 14,350 tons, 28,000 h.p., speed 23 knots; carries 400 first and 205 second class passengers

econd class passengers

tar Liner, "Teutonic" (1889)

ons, 16,000 h.p., speed 20 knots; carries 300 first and 190 second class passengers

The Cunarder, "Campania" (1893)

Built on the Clyde; 600 ft. long, 12,950 tons, 28,000 h.p., speed 22 knots; carries 400 first and 300 second and 600 third class passengers

DRAWN BY A. B. CULL

advertized and competed for the same cargoes and passengers. Common sense held that it would be better for business to have the three ships leave on different days. In fact, it would be ideal if a major liner could leave New York *every* day carrying cargo, passengers and mail. In driving down the price of a third-class passage to America—at one point to as little as £2—Morgan hoped to create a virtual monopoly in the North Atlantic. The only major fly in the ointment was Cunard.

Cunard the entrepreneur

Samuel Cunard was born in Halifax, Nova Scotia, in 1787, the son of Abraham Cunard, a foreman carpenter with the British army. The Cunard family were well known for their thriftiness and for having an eye for a good investment. Although Abraham's role with the army precluded him from involving himself in external businesses, he slowly built up a portfolio of property near the docks in Halifax, acquiring access rights to the shore on his investments near the harbor in order to build wharves. Not only did he prosper from the rents he charged on his properties, but he was also able to make a tidy profit from those ships landing cargo at his wharves. Samuels's connection with maritime trade, therefore, was established in his early years when he and his brother (he also had seven sisters) bought goods at the wharves that they then sold at market in town. They also sold vegetables from the family plot at the market, and while tending the family cow at pasture, frugal Samuel is famous for having been seen knitting socks as the animal grazed. By the time he was 17, Samuel was managing his own general store, but it wasn't long before he became involved in the timber business, launching his career as an entrepreneurial exporter and importer.

Samuel involved himself in all aspects of the businesses he set up, even acting as auctioneer at his own warehouse, built on his own wharf, to sell the chests of tea he had imported from China. He had amassed a considerable fortune by the time he was in his early thirties, running a shipping line with around 40 vessels, and was one of the most influential men in Nova Scotia. In 1838 he crossed the Atlantic to enter into negotiations for the lucrative transatlantic mail contract about to be offered for

tender by Her Majesty's government. Because the contract was for a steamship service, Cunard formed the British and North American Royal Mail Steam Packet Company—even though he didn't own a single steamship. Cunard won the contract partly by promising that he would guarantee regular sailings, even during the stormy winter months. Mindful of the severe penalties for failing to maintain a regular schedule with punctual service, other shipping magnates against whom he was competing for the contract shied away.

Cunard's first steamship, the paddle steamer *Britannia*, crossed the Atlantic from Liverpool to Boston in 1840, albeit with its steam engines augmented by a substantial array of sails. Thereafter, Cunard expanded his shipping line with the addition of, among others, his first iron-hulled, screw-propeller-driven ship, the *Andes*, in 1852. Samuel Cunard was knighted by Queen Victoria for his services to the British maritime industry in 1859, and he died six years later in 1865.

The Cunard Line, as his shipping company was then known, grew to become the most innovative and respected shipping line in the world, being the first to introduce electric lighting and wireless communications on board its ships. By 1870 the White Star Line, which had previously traded on the Australian route with wooden-hulled sailing vessels, launched the iron-hulled *Oceanic,* built specifically for service as a passenger liner in the North Atlantic. At the time, Cunard was operating around two dozen cargo and passenger vessels on the North Atlantic as well as in the Mediterranean. His dominant position on the transatlantic route was, however, far from unassailable. Within the space of a year, White Star was to follow the 3,707-ton *Oceanic* with her sister ships the *Atlantic*, *Baltic* and *Republic*. The following year came the larger *Celtic* and *Adriatic*, and by 1875 there were a dozen White Star liners. Not all of these were intended exclusively for the North Atlantic—White Star also sailed to the Middle East, India, the Far East and Australia—but two in particular provided serious competition for Cunard. The *Britannia* and *Germanic* could both maintain 16 knots, a speed that allowed them to cross the Atlantic in comfortably less than eight days. The time taken to cross the Atlantic was fast becoming a hotly contested issue.

Far left: Sir Samuel Cunard was an entrepreneur from Canada, who, in 1838, won the contract to provide a transatlantic steamship service carrying the Royal Mail despite the fact that, at that time, he did not own even one steamship. Cunard was knighted by Queen Victoria in 1859 and died in 1865 at the age of 78.

Left: Born into a banking family in Hartford, Connecticut, in 1837, J. P. Morgan became the most powerful financier in America, leading a group that saved the U.S. government from bankruptcy in 1895 and preventing a Wall Street crash in 1907. He died in 1913.

The Blue Riband contest

The much coveted Blue Riband, an honor for which the different shipping lines competed, allowed the ship that achieved the fastest crossing of the Atlantic to fly a blue pennant from her mast. Both the ship that held the Blue Riband and the shipping line that owned the Blue Riband holder earned a great deal of publicity. It was a matter of immense pride and huge prestige to be able to market the ship or company that provided the fastest passage across the Atlantic. The little blue pennant fluttering from the masthead, therefore, represented hard currency—dollars and cents, pounds and shillings—in revenue from ticket sales and cargo contracts.

Cunard had first held the Blue Riband as early as 1840 when the Britannia crossed from New York at an average speed of just over 10 knots, a journey time of just under 10 days. At that time, the Blue Riband may not have meant quite as much as it did 20 years later, when steam was completely overpowering sail and the Atlantic waters were churning with competition on scheduled steamship services. By then, the Blue Riband was a trophy to be flown in the face of the opposition, a banner to wave that said you were the fastest and the best—and you had proved it. Different records were set and broken for both east- and westbound crossings, but a glance at the history of the westbound Blue Riband shows how keenly contested it

was. Although the honor changed hands several times up to 1856, Cunard held it from then, through the efforts of the Persia and the Scotia, up until 1872, when the new White Star liner Adriatic achieved an average speed of over 14.5 knots—a crossing time just a few minutes short of eight days. Three years later White Star's *Germanic* took the average speed up to 14.65 knots, and although Inman Lines' City of Berlin briefly took the record in 1875, White Star retained the honor through *Britannia* and *Germanic* for the next six years.

In 1882 another British company, the Guion Line, was able to offer its passengers the fastest Atlantic crossing on its steamers the *Alaska* and *Oregon*. Guion's ships took the crossing time to under seven days for the first time, with the *Oregon* raising the average speed to 18.56 knots. The *Oregon* was sold to Cunard in 1884, the same year that Cunard's *Etruria* made the crossing at 18.73 knots in just six days five and a half hours. The *Etruria* broke her own record in 1888 with an average speed of 19.56 knots and, along with her sister ship, the *Umbria*, held the Blue Riband until 1889, when the Inman Lines' *City of Paris* took the crossing time to under six days. Inman Lines was by this time known as Inman & International and was part of the American International Navigation Company. However, the *City of Paris* was still operating under a British flag when she broke her own record

and raised the average speed for a crossing from Queenstown, in Ireland, to a fraction over 20 knots. In 1891 White Star's *Majestic* and *Teutonic* achieved average speeds of 20.1 and 20.35 knots, making the crossing from Queenstown in just 5 days, 16 hours and 35 minutes. The *City of Paris* snatched the record back in 1892, but Cunard reclaimed the title when the *Campania* and *Lucania* took the average speed up to just under 22 knots in 1893, maintaining their position as the fastest transatlantic liners for the next five years. It was then that the unthinkable happened.

Being forced to relinquish the Blue Riband now and again to one of the other British lines wasn't a position Cunard relished, but at least the trophy was being held safe in British hands. Other Blue Riband liners flew the Union Jack just as the Cunarders did and sharing the honor with other British-built ships showed that Queen Victoria's empire was sustained by the finest merchant navy in the world. British technology and

Launched in 1907, a year after *Lusitania*, the Royal Navy's most advanced warship was HMS *Bellerophon*, yet she could achieve only 21 knots, making her around 5 knots slower than the *Cunarder*.

British engineering produced the fastest, most advanced ships on the high seas. Truly, Britannia ruled the waves. The Germans, however, had other ideas.

In November 1897 the Norddeutscher-Lloyd (NDL) liner *Kaiser Wilhelm der Grosse* set a new record average speed of 22.33 knots for an eastbound crossing and four months later took the westbound record at 22.29 knots. For the first time since the *Great Western* made the crossing 60 years before, the Blue Riband flew from the mast of a ship that did not also fly the Union Jack. The British, who had prided themselves on being the world's foremost maritime nation for centuries, took it as a huge affront to national pride that the Blue Riband had been lost to the Germans. Cunard was especially aggrieved. The Cunarders could be forgiven for having come to believe that the Blue Riband rightfully belonged to them alone. They had held the record for no less than 25 of the previous 42 years. But the *Kaiser Wilhelm* wasn't only proclaiming its superiority in terms of speed. NDL advertised it as the largest ship afloat, at almost 1,000 tons more than the *Lucania* and 20 ft. (6 m) longer. Despite being bigger, she carried almost 250 fewer passengers—800 third-class (or "steerage"), 370 second-class and 590 first-class. This also led to NDL claiming that the *Kaiser Wilhelm* was the most spacious and luxurious liner in the world, a claim that was backed up by the acres of polished wood and sumptuous furnishings.

While providing a demeaning slap in the face for Cunard, the *Kaiser Wilhelm* also demonstrated how ships were becoming bigger as well as faster. Compared with Cunard's *Etruria*, launched just 12 years previously, the *Kaiser Wilhelm* had a displacement that was 6,000 tons greater, was over 100 feet longer and could accommodate more than 400 extra passengers. Brunel's *Great Britain* of 1843, once the largest ship afloat, had been just 3,200 tons, carrying only 120 first-class and 132 second-class passengers. Brunel's idea, however, that steamships would provide economies of scale, with bigger most definitely meaning better, was now being proved beyond a shadow of a doubt.

The Hamburg-America Line, also known as Hapag, shared in Germany's glory when its liner *Deutschland* increased the average speed for a westbound Atlantic crossing to just over 23 knots in 1900. The *Deutschland* lost the title to NDL's *Kronprinz Wilhelm* in 1902 but grabbed it back in 1903. The Germans were to hold on to the Blue Riband for the next four years until the arrival of a ship that heralded a whole new breed of superliner.

Britain sailed into the twentieth century with its domination of the North Atlantic passenger trade routes under serious threat. Not only were the Germans crossing the Atlantic faster but many of Britain's finest ships were no longer actually British. In 1902 J. P. Morgan's IMMC bought the Leyland Line for $11 million, the Dominion Line for $4.5 million and the White Star

Line for $32 million. Today this would represent an investment of many billions of dollars—the sort of investment that sends shock waves through the stock markets and forces governments to take an interest. Takeovers on this scale can affect people's livelihoods, the shape of an industry, the economy of the country and politicians' jobs. More than that, shipping is the lifeline to the outside world for an island nation such as Great Britain, and in times of war the merchant marine plays a vital role as part of the military.

Military matters

During the Crimean War in 1853, most of Cunard's fleet was commandeered by the British Admiralty to be used as troop ships and both Cunard and White Star liners were used to ferry troops to and from South Africa during the Boer War of 1899–1902. The Admiralty needed to rely on being able to requisition ships flying the British flag, operated by British companies and with British crews. The potential for disastrous security breaches and the infiltration of spies and saboteurs if too many foreigners were involved was obvious.

There was also another military factor to be taken into consideration. The new German ships had the potential to be converted in time of war into armed cruisers capable of causing havoc among merchant vessels or supply convoys, and able to outrun most naval vessels. The Royal Navy's most advanced warship, HMS *Bellerophon*, due to be launched in 1907, was not expected to achieve more than 21 knots. The Royal Navy had to show that it could counter the threat posed by the German liners by deploying its own armed cruisers. For economic and military reasons as well as national pride, therefore, the British government and the Admiralty saw its relationship with Cunard as being more valuable than ever. Cunard, however, was embroiled in a vicious commercial battle with the IMMC, as J. P. Morgan was determined either to buy them out or wipe them out to achieve an Atlantic monopoly.

While trade agreements prevented the British government from stepping in to offer direct support to Cunard or to subsidize its commercial operations, in 1903 Cunard's chairman, Lord Inverclyde, put forward a proposal that would

SECOND CLASS
SMOKE ROOM

2nd CLASS
PROMENADE
+ LOUNGE

SECOND CABIN
DINING SALOON (on
SALOON DECK)

VERANDAH
+ CAFÉ

SALOON
SMOKE ROOM

SALOON LOU...
ROOM
1st C. DINING

BOAT DECK

PROMENADE
DECK

SALOON DECK

MAIN DECK

FIREMAN'S QUARTERS

STEERING GEAR

MAILS

ENGINES

GO AHEAD
TURBINE

ASTERN
TURBINE

STARTER
PLATFORM

FRESH WATER TANKS

100 FT.

Controversy and conspiracy theories still surround the sinking of the *Lusitania* by a German submarine during the First World War. She may have been secretly carrying ammunition supplied illegally by the then neutral United States. This could have made her a "legitimate" target for the U-boat. Nevertheless, 1,200 passengers died in the tragedy.

MAIN STAIRCASE & ELEVATORS
1ST CLASS NURSERY
WIRELESS
1ST CLASS LIBRARY
OFFICERS' ROOMS
NAVIGATING BRIDGE
CAPTAIN'S ROOMS
BOAT DECK
PROMENADE DECK
UPPER DECK
SALOON DECK
MAIN DECK
REFRIGERATED
FRESH WATER
COAL
CARGO
CHAIN LOCKER
CARGO
BOILERS

THE POINT AT WHICH THE TORPEDO STRUCK VESSEL

The Cunard liner *Carmania*, launched in 1905, was fitted with new turbine engines as an experiment. Her sister ship, *Caronia*, was fitted with traditional reciprocating engines. In service, *Carmania* was faster and burned less fuel, so the decision was taken that the next generation of Cunarders, *Lusitania* and *Mauretania*, should be turbine-powered.

appeal to both the government and his company. To compete with the Germans and with the White Star Line, Inverclyde needed two new ships for Cunard—two new ships that were bigger, faster and more luxurious than anything ever built. All he needed from the government was a loan. The loan, however, had to be at a very special rate—2.75 percent over 20 years. It was also for a very special amount—£2.6 million. That may not sound like much for a government to spend nowadays, but 100 years later, at the beginning of the twenty-first century, a similar ship was built—for £550 million. It was the *Queen Mary II*, the biggest, most luxurious, fastest, most expensive transatlantic liner in the world. The £2.6 million Lord Inverclyde asked for represents the cost of building today two *Queen Mary IIs*. In return for the loan, Cunard would ensure that the vessels were made available to the Admiralty whenever they were required, to be used as armed cruisers, troop ships or hospital ships.

The idea of the British government helping to fund the building of ships in return for the ships being called into service by the Admiralty in times of crisis was not a new one. The White Star liners *Teutonic* and *Majestic*, for example, had both been built with government grants 20 years before. It was the scale of Lord Inverclyde's proposal and the huge amount of money involved that made it so audacious.

Special stipulations

The government agreed but had a few stipulations to make. No doubt Lord Inverclyde had expected this. The Admiralty had always had certain requirements for mail ships, with which Cunard had been happy to comply. They had agreed, for example, that their mail ships' crews should include among their number at least one officer of the Royal Navy with the power to take over the ship to protect the Royal Mail should the need arise. In effect, most of the "mail" officers were expected to do little more than enjoy the trip. The government's requirements for the new ships were extensive and precise, extending not only to the building and operating of the ships but also to the running of the Cunard Line and all of its other ships.

The new ships had to be able to maintain an average speed in moderate weather of 24–25 knots, and all plans and designs were to be approved by the Admiralty. Construction of the ships was to come under the scrutiny of an independent inspector to ensure that the specifications were being adhered to rigidly. In addition, provisions had to be made for the installation of "fittings" that would prepare the ships for military use, with storage provided for such fittings, and the stored fittings had to be properly maintained. Cunard further undertook to maintain a mail service once a week from Liverpool via Queenstown to New York, leaving on a Saturday, and promised that the usual provisions for facilities such as a mail-sorting office would be made on any vessel that was used to carry the mail. They were not to supply any vessel on charter except to the Indian government, and none of the company's ships capable of 17 knots or more could be sold without the government's approval.

The agreement required that all of Cunard's vessels be kept seaworthy and ready for inspection, as all of them would be at the disposal of the Admiralty whenever they were required. All vessels had to be registered under a British flag, and all company steamship masters, officers and at least 75 percent of the crew had to be British. The company as a whole had to remain under British control, all company directors and senior managers had to be British, and no shares were to be sold to foreigners or foreign companies. And there was more—the clauses and subclauses covering Cunard's obligations under the agreement punctuated the contract like rivets on a ship's hull. Lord Inverclyde had avoided being boarded or sunk by the pirate J. P. Morgan; instead, he'd been coerced by the navy. Taking the king's shilling, however, meant that Cunard could now begin work on building the world's most advanced ships.

Lord Inverclyde needed the new liners in service as quickly as possible, so the construction contracts were awarded to two separate shipyards. The John Brown yard at Clydebank was chosen for the first ship, the *Lusitania*, while her sister ship, the *Mauretania*, was to be built in Newcastle by Swan, Hunter and Wigham Richardson. The ships' romantic names were exactly that—Roman. The *Lusitania* was named after Roman Portugal, and the *Mauretania* after Roman Morocco. That air of romance was also to be integral to the design of the ships' interiors, intended from the outset to be distinctly different, affording each ship its own individual character. (Exactly the opposite approach was adopted by the White Star Line when the *Olympic* and *Titanic* were fitted out a few years later, as they decided on a more uniform look that made both ships immediately identifiable as sisters.) Further adding to the differences between the new Cunarders, the shipyards competed with one another to add their own refinements, with the approval of the owners, each hoping to build the biggest, fastest and best of the sister ships.

The *Lusitania* was the first to be completed. Her keel plates were laid down in June 1904, and two years later she was ready for launch. She was over 785 ft. (239 m) long, more than 150 ft. (45 m) longer than the *Kaiser Wilhelm der Grosse*. Lady Inverclyde broke a bottle of Champagne over the *Lusitania*'s bow, watched by around 20,000 spectators. Sadly, Lord Inverclyde did not live to see the launch of his superliner—he died in 1905 when only 44 years of age. The *Lusitania* was to spend an additional year being fitted out. She was divided into 34 separate watertight compartments, which were believed to make her virtually unsinkable, and she had 192 furnaces to heat the 27 boilers that provided her steam power.

The steam, however, was not driving the normal type of reciprocating engine but rather the largest steam turbines ever built. Instead of installing the conventional style of steamship engines, where steam from the boilers expands in giant pistons that pump up and down to turn a shaft (much as the pistons in a modern car engine do), Cunard decided to go for the new turbine designs. They had tested turbine engines in a smaller ship, the *Carmania*, which had been launched in 1905. The *Carmania*'s sister ship, the *Caronia*, was fitted with traditional reciprocating steam "piston" engines, and the performances of the two otherwise identical ships were compared. The *Carmania* was more efficient, using less fuel and achieving higher speeds than the

Caronia. The decision was made. The new Cunarders would be fitted with turbine engines.

Turbulent turbine power

Turbines are engines whereby steam from the boilers is fed at high pressure over the blades of a turbine, forcing them to turn like the sails of a windmill and thus spin the propeller shaft. They were far more expensive to produce because they had to be built using more costly materials and highly advanced engineering technology. Nevertheless, the potential savings in fuel costs, the greater power output and resultant higher speed were well worth the initial investment. Theoretically, the smoother operation of the turbines' rotating motion— transferring power to the spinning propeller shaft with greater ease than the reciprocal engines' pumping motion, should have caused far less vibration throughout the ship and provided a more relaxing environment for the passengers. Unfortunately, this was not the case in practice and, when the *Lusitania* set out on her sea trials, violent shuddering was experienced in her stern section at high speed. Her entire stern had to be gutted and fitted with extra bracing beams to try to counter the problem. The 142 second-class cabins were torn apart, causing a month's delay in her completion.

Finally, she was handed over to Cunard, who opened her to the public in September 1907 in Southampton, allowing thousands of visitors to come aboard and marvel at the combination of craftsmanship and technology. The plasterwork, decorated with gold leaf, that had been used by the designer James Millar to create a Georgian or Louis XVI-style interior décor in the public areas, was lit in breathtaking fashion by electric lights. Other electrical equipment like the elevators, fans and clocks that were plugged into the *Lusitania*'s 300

Lord Inverclyde, chairman of the Cunard Line, was the driving force behind the unprecedented deal with the British government that saw his shipping company receive preferential loans for the building of the *Lusitania* and *Mauretania*. Unfortunately, he died in 1905 at the age of just 44, one year before *Lusitania*'s launch.

miles (483 kilometers) of electric wiring, gave the undeniable impression that this was a thoroughly modern ship while the classically carved oak chairs and tables might have graced the most elegant of London's finest hotels. The *Lusitania* was, in fact, a 31,550-ton floating hotel capable of accommodating more than 2,000 guests. No lumbering giant, within a month of entering service, *Lusitania* brought the Blue Riband back to Cunard. She subsequently lost it but to her sister ship, the *Mauretania*, that raised the average Atlantic crossing speed to 26 knots, cutting the journey time to just under four and a half days. It was a record the *Mauretania* would hold from 1909 until 1929. Tragically, the *Lusitania* was torpedoed by a German U-boat in 1915 and sank with the loss of almost 1,200 lives.

The *Lusitania* and *Mauretania* reestablished Cunard as the leading shipping line in the North Atlantic. Not only had they produced the world's largest ships, showcasing the skills, ingenuity and technical prowess of British craftsmen as well as the superiority of British industry, they had humbled the haughty Germans in the bargain. With increasing political tension between the two nations—tension that would erupt into war seven years later—the Cunarders were lauded as national champions. The swell of nationalist fervor elevated the Cunard Line, in the eyes of the great patriotic British public, to the position of being "Britain's" shipping line—the pride of the nation. But that pride was not necessarily shared by all of King Edward VII's subjects.

Birth of the *Titanic*

On a midsummer evening in 1907, Mr. Joseph Bruce Ismay and his wife, Florence, arrived in Belgrave Square, whose residents were among the wealthiest people in Britain, having been invited to dinner at Downshire House, the London residence of Lord and Lady Pirrie. Lord Pirrie and Ismay were close business associates. Pirrie was the chairman of Harland & Wolff in Belfast, one of the largest shipbuilders in the world, and Ismay was the chairman of the White Star Line as well as president and managing director of the IMMC. Each had a vital financial interest in the other's business, which had led to all White Star Line ships being built in Belfast; each was also gravely

Part of Belgrave Square in London in the early 1900s. Most of the grand buildings were, at that time, private residences. A century later the buildings have mostly been turned into embassies or institutions since their size and the cost of their upkeep make them impractical as modern family homes.

concerned about the impact of the publicity that the new Cunarders, now nicknamed "ocean greyhounds," were enjoying.

It was not considered to be good form to dwell on business matters at the dinner table, but afterwards the two had much to discuss. Ismay was determined that the White Star Line, long having prided itself on operating the finest ships of any transatlantic fleet by providing its passengers with the ultimate in luxury travel, should not be openly relegated to the status of an "also ran" in the eyes of the British public by the patriotic hysteria generated by the successes of the *Lusitania* and *Mauretania*. In Ismay's eyes Cunard did not deserve to be regarded as the premier British shipping line—White Star ships still flew the Union Jack, after all, even though they were now owned by the IMMC and no longer as truly British as Cunard. The IMMC and J. P. Morgan had continued to run the shipping lines under subsidiary companies based in their home countries so that they could fly their own national flags and benefit from the national loyalties of passengers who wanted to travel on their own countries' ships. All of that loyalty and national pride now appeared to have been hijacked by Cunard. If things continued in this vein, it was easy to see how Cunard would come to be the principal player in transatlantic shipping.

Lord Pirrie, of course, fully understood how that situation would affect Harland & Wolff. A significant downturn in business for White Star would mean that new orders would dry up, spelling disaster for the Belfast shipyard. Although it might at first have seemed that the solution would be to cross the Atlantic faster than the Cunarders and take the Blue Riband from them, this was neither desirable nor practical. The pursuit of speed had never really been a priority for White Star. Elegance and luxury were their watchwords, and it had never been White Star's policy to conquer the Atlantic in terms of speed alone despite the fact that they had held the Blue Riband many times in the past. In any case, winning the Blue Riband from Cunard could never generate as much enthusiasm or fire the emotions of the British public to the extent that it had done when Cunard took the honor from the Germans. There was also a practical problem in going for speed: White Star's fastest ships—the *Teutonic*, *Oceanic* and *Adriatic*—could only achieve 21 knots, whereas the Cunarders could achieve 26. Making them faster would mean reducing cargo and passenger space to install new equipment. That would never be financially viable.

Building a new liner that could compete was really the only option, but the only way to be absolutely sure of outstripping the "greyhounds" was to build a ship with bigger, better, more powerful turbines than those of the Cunarders! The more conventional type of reciprocating engine simply could not produce the same kind of performance. But new turbines could take years and enormous amounts of money to develop—money that might better be spent on other aspects of a new ship, especially as the two men would not benefit from the sort of deal the late Lord Inverclyde had struck with the government. During their lengthy discussion the two explored all of the avenues open to them, ultimately concluding that their most sensible route was to do what the White Star Line had always prided itself upon—be the best.

Ships for the superrich

There was no real need to involve the White Star Line in a futile race for the Blue Riband; no need to stray from company policy in that respect. They would simply build the biggest, most luxurious, safest, most impressive oceangoing vessel the world had ever seen. They would build a ship that would be as graceful and elegant as the room in which they were sitting, but this would be beauty on a grand scale—a ship to be envied by shipping lines and maritime nations the world over. Naturally, it would have to earn its keep, but they had little doubt that they would be able to attract customers. The passenger trade across the Atlantic hadn't been so buoyant for years.

Toward the end of the nineteenth century, the Inman Line had sent over 3,000 agents into Europe to sell passages to the relatives of immigrants already in America, and by 1907, despite ever more stringent U.S. government immigration restrictions, more immigrants than ever before entered America—1.25 million through Ellis Island alone. These passengers did not travel in the most luxurious accommodations—they were third-, or "steerage" class—but a full complement of third-class passengers at the right fare could pay for enough coal to take a liner to New York and back again. There was also the mail subsidy to consider. No deal could ever be as good as the one Cunard had secured, but there was still money to be made in transporting the Royal Mail. The new liner would carry a certain amount of cargo, too, but the real profit was to be earned from those most affluent of travelers who were able to afford the most exquisite accommodations, the most sumptuously appointed cabins, the most attentive service. Ismay and Pirrie had to make their new liner the only choice of travel for the Edwardian superrich.

With this plan they would need at least two ships to maintain a proper transatlantic service—or why not three? That, after all, was how the *Teutonic*, *Adriatic* and *Oceanic* operated, as a kind of Atlantic shuttle service. Ismay and Pirrie set to work sketching out some ideas on paper that very night. They produced rough drawings of how the new ships might look, also deciding that they should have names reflecting their status as the mightiest liners ever built—the *Olympic*, *Titanic* and *Gigantic*.

Following the demise of the *Titanic*, shipbuilding at Harland & Wolff in Belfast might have been expected to be badly affected. On the contrary, the shipyard went on to build ever bigger and more modern vessels. The *Stirling Castle* is seen here in the dry dock in 1935.

CHAPTER TWO

WHO BUILT THE *TITANIC*?

Lord Pirrie took the concept sketches and design ideas roughed out by himself and Ismay to Belfast, where a number of key men would turn their ideas into solid steel reality. People had been building ships of one kind or another around the shores of Belfast Lough for as long as men had lived there, and even the "modern" industry that Lord Pirrie knew could trace its history back almost 250 years. In all that time, nothing approaching the size of the new ships he now presented to his design team had ever been attempted, not even by the mighty Harland & Wolff.

The company's history stretched back to 1791 and the beginning of the modern era of shipbuilding in Belfast, when an enterprising Scottish shipbuilder named William Ritchie saw the work of the Belfast Harbour Commission in straightening the River Lagan. The modern port facilities that were planned seemed ideal for supporting a new business venture, and Ritchie applied for permission to establish a boat repair yard. Before long, he was not only repairing boats but also building them, and within 20 years he had expanded his company from a workforce of just 10 men to well over 100. Ritchie's brother, Hugh, eventually set up another shipyard on the Lagan with his partner, Alastair McLaine and in 1820 launched the very first Irish-built steamship, the *Belfast*. More shipyards were to follow until in 1851 the Harbour Commission gave permission for the development of a new site on Queen's Island.

The island had been formed when the Harbour Commission dug a "canal" to cut out a bend in the river during their ongoing program of improvement. Water still flowed round the shallow bend, isolating the land that was to become Queen's Island (later, the "bend" would be filled in, making Queen's Island technically no longer an island). The first shipbuilder on Queen's Island was the small firm of Thompson & Kirwan, to be followed by another, two years later, when Robert Hickson established the first yard dedicated to the building of iron-hulled ships. Almost immediately Hickson advertised for a shipyard manager, and the man who got the job was a young engineer named Edward James Harland.

Born in Scarborough in May 1831, Harland was the son of a doctor who took a keen interest in all things mechanical and who was happy for his son to become apprenticed at the engineering works of Robert Stephenson in Newcastle-upon-Tyne. In 1851 Harland moved to Glasgow to work for J & G Thompson, who built marine engines. He spent two years there before moving back to Tyneside as a manager at the Thomas Toward yard. His return to Tyneside lasted only a year before he moved to Belfast at the age of 23 to become Robert Hickson's shipyard manager. The young Harland was given a rough ride in Belfast to begin with, having to deal with wage disputes, supply problems and general industrial unrest in a business that was far from flourishing. He needed help to get the business back on its feet, and on the advice of an old friend, the German entrepreneur Gustav Schwabe (who had financial interests in shipping with the Bibby Line of Liverpool), Harland employed Schwabe's nephew, Gustav Wolff, as his assistant.

Gustav Wilhelm Wolff, born in Hamburg in November 1834, was the son of a German businessman. He began his education in Germany but was sent to Liverpool College at the age of 14, joining the Manchester engineering firm of Joseph Whitworth & Co. two years later as an apprentice. He also worked as an engineering draftsman for another company before being hired by Harland in 1857. The two men worked hard to breathe new life into the business, but by 1858 it was clear that Hickson wanted to bow out of shipbuilding and he offered to sell the entire yard to Harland for £5,000.

Harland & Wolff emerges

Again, seeking the advice of his old friend, Harland discussed the offer with Gustav Schwabe, who not only encouraged him to take the offer but also provided the financing to make it possible for Harland to buy out Hickson. Gustav Wolff then proved his worth not only as a draftsman and manager but also as a businessman when he was instrumental in securing an order from the Bibby Line for three new ships. The new liners were to be called the *Venetian*, *Sicilian* and *Syrian*. Launched in 1859, the *Venetian* was listed (and is still listed) as vessel No. 1 in Harland & Wolff's order book. Gustav Wolff became Harland's partner in 1860, the year that the *Sicilian* and *Syrian* (Nos. 2 and 3 in the order book) were launched, and in 1861 the company officially changed its name to become Harland & Wolff.

Although his father was an Ulsterman, William Pirrie was born in Canada, like the shipping magnate Samuel Cunard. He was brought to County Down as a baby and started work at Harland & Wolff as a premium apprentice when he was just 15. He succeeded Sir Edward Harland as chairman of the company 33 years later.

The rise of Lord Pirrie

William James Pirrie was born in Quebec, Canada, in 1847. His father, an Ulsterman, died when his son was still only a baby and his mother, Eliza, took William home to County Down, where he spent his childhood in Conlig, near Bangor. As a boy, he went to primary school in Belfast before attending the Belfast Royal Academical Institute. From there he went to Harland & Wolff, where, as a premium apprentice, he was treated as a management trainee, moving from department to department but working principally as a draftsman. By 1869 he was held in such high regard by the senior management at the yard that he was appointed chief designer on the yard's prestigious new vessel, the *Oceanic*. In 1874, at the age of just 27, Pirrie was made a partner at Harland & Wolff. His boundless energy and enthusiasm saw him at the yard, where he involved himself in all aspects of the business, from early in the morning until late into the evening. Ambitious and forceful, Pirrie was determined to maneuvre himself into positions of ever greater authority at the shipyard. He genuinely enjoyed being involved in all aspects of the business, reveling in the excitement of working on state-of-the-art vessels, ships that incorporated all of the latest, most modern technological developments—ships that were bigger, better and faster than ever before.

In 1879 Pirrie married Margaret Montgomery Carlisle, the sister of one of Harland & Wolff's foremost designers, Alexander Carlisle. When Pirrie took over from Sir Edward Harland as chairman of Harland & Wolff, the Pirries also bought Ormiston House, a large, imposing mansion in East Belfast where Harland lived until his death on Christmas Eve 1895. Ormiston was surrounded by extensive garden grounds with views down to Queen's Island and the Harland & Wolff yards, and it was there in 1897 that Pirrie, by then Lord Mayor of Belfast, played host to the Duke and Duchess of York, inviting thousands of Sunday school children to meet his guests. As well as becoming Lord Mayor of Belfast, Pirrie also served on the Harbour Commission and was made a baron in 1906.

Lord and Lady Pirrie enjoyed the comfort of Downshire House when they were in London, but they also owned Witley Park, a mansion set in 14,000 acres (567 hectares) in Surrey.

Harland married Rosa Wann of Vermont, Belfast, in 1860. He became chairman of the Harbour Commission and was also involved in politics, standing as mayor of Belfast in 1885 and 1886, when he was created a baron. Three years later he was elected as the MP for the Northern Division of Belfast and was reelected in 1892 and 1895. Like Sir Edward Harland, Gustav Wolff also became involved in politics and served as the MP for East Belfast from his election in 1892 until his retirement eight years later. He had a house in Strandtown, Belfast, although in the latter part of his life, he spent less and less time in Ulster and died in London in 1913. Sir Edward Harland remained involved with Harland & Wolff until his death in 1895. The role of chairman of the company was taken by William James Pirrie.

Pirrie began his career at Harland & Wolff in 1862 at the age of 15, hired by a company that then had only around 100 employees as a premium or "gentleman" apprentice. Such an apprenticeship had to be bought, with the the apprentice's parents paying up to £100 to secure the position. This made the premium apprenticeship attainable only by well-educated, middle-class boys, as the price represented more than a year's wages for a skilled working-class tradesman and around three months' salary for a qualified professional such as an engineer.

Part of the *Stirling Castle*'s rudder stock is hoisted into place in 1935 from the flatbed of a Harkness & Co. wagon. Harkness was a local hauler that transported much of the heavy equipment for installation on the *Titanic*.

Lord Pirrie was a man of great wealth and influence by the time he and Joseph Bruce Ismay conceived of the Olympic-class liners. Ismay, too, although he was 15 years younger than the master shipbuilder, was a man of some substance. These were not two woolly-headed dreamers conjuring up some fanciful scheme to build the world's biggest ship. Both knew precisely what they were doing. Lord Pirrie had many years of experience in building world-renowned ships, and Ismay was in charge of the most powerful shipping organization on the planet. The two also had a unique understanding that stemmed from the longstanding relationship between Harland & Wolff and the White Star Line.

Formed in 1845, the White Star Line had operated sailing ships to the Far East and Australia during the Australian gold rush. But when gold fever subsided, so, too, did the fortunes of the White Star Line. The shipping company went into liquidation with debts of more than £500,00 and was bought up by Thomas Ismay in 1868. Ismay, the son of a shipbuilder, had started his working life in the 1850s as an apprentice at the Liverpool shipbrokers Imrie, Tomlinson & Co., but had big plans to create a steamship company. In partnership with William Imrie, Ismay set up the Oceanic Steam Navigation Company, buying the White Star Line's name and flag for £1,000, a deal that was financed by the German entrepreneur Gustav Schwabe. Schwabe and Ismay agreed that as part of the deal, the new company's new ships would be built at the Belfast shipyard of Schwabe's nephew, Gustav Wolff. From then on, the futures of White Star and Harland & Wolff were forged together, since White Star's new ships would be paid for partly in cash and partly in White Star Line shares. Harland & Wolff, therefore, came to own a large interest in the White Star Line over subsequent years.

The first ship ordered by White Star was the *Oceanic*, one of the first of a new breed of ocean liners. Built on a grand scale, *Oceanic* was not only large but also thoroughly modern. Harland & Wolff had designed the *Oceanic* differently from most previous ships, with the superstructure combined as part of the hull rather than simply bolted on to the deck. Other modern passenger conveniences, such as running water in all of her

cabins, made the *Oceanic* truly remarkable, and these qualities of innovation and luxury were to become the proud hallmark of the White Star ships built by Harland & Wolff. By the time Thomas Ismay's eldest son, Joseph, joined his father's business, the White Star Line was thriving and had established an enviable reputation for the opulence of its passenger accommodations.

Joseph Bruce Ismay

Joseph was certainly no stranger to the White Star fleet. Born in 1862, he was brought up in a house looking out over the River Mersey as it flows into the Irish Sea. The White Star ships were easy for young Joseph to spot—they were the ones that sounded their horns in salute as they passed his house! The family later moved to a mansion Thomas Ismay had built in the Wirral. Educated at Elstree School and Harrow, J. Bruce Ismay, as he is usually known, worked for the White Star Line in New York, where during the 1880s, he cut quite a figure in society circles.

In 1888 he was married to Julia Florence Schieffelin in New York, a wedding that no one in high society would have wanted to miss. The ceremony was held at the Church of the Heavenly Rest on Fifth Avenue. The bride was resplendent in a gown of white brocade trimmed with old point lace, her lace veil was held in place by a diamond tiara and a diamond pendant hung from a perfect string of pearls around her neck. After the ceremony the reception was held at the bride's parents' residence on East Forty-ninth Street and the newlyweds seemed destined to enjoy a privileged and affluent New York lifestyle. Their first daughter, Florence, was born in 1889, and she was followed by a son, Henry. Sadly, Henry fared badly during a stiflingly hot summer in New York in 1891, suffering chronic diarrhea and other ailments that prompted the Ismays' doctor to advise that he be taken away from the sweltering   city, with an ocean voyage hopefully helping to restore his health. The family traveled to Liverpool on the *Teutonic*, but Henry's condition grew worse and he died shortly after arriving in England.

The Ismays settled in Liverpool in a mansion called Sandheys at Mossley Hill, from where J. Bruce would walk the 4 miles (6 kilometers) to the White Star offices in Water Street. In 1896

Far left: Joseph Bruce Ismay succeeded his father, Thomas, as chairman of the White Star Line in 1899 at the age of 37. He presided over the sale of White Star to the IMMC and, five years after the takeover, J. Bruce Ismay was chairman the IMMC and one of the most powerful shipping magnates in the world.

Left: Thomas Andrews joined Harland & Wolff as a premium apprentice in 1889. By the time the *Titanic* was taking shape in 1910, Andrews was in charge of Harland & Wolff's design department.

the company moved into a brand-new building nearby on the corner of James Street and the Strand designed by the architect R. N. Shaw, who had also been responsible for Scotland Yard's new headquarters in London. On November 23, 1899, Thomas Ismay died at his mansion, Dawpool, and was buried at the nearby Thurstaston cemetery. J. Bruce Ismay succeeded his father as chairman of the White Star Line and within a year was in negotiations with J. P. Morgan for the sale of the company. This is not to suggest that Thomas Ismay's beloved White Star Line was sold off as soon as he was gone—this was a matter of remaining competitive in a very competitive market. Ismay, along with Lord Pirrie, who was a major White Star shareholder in his own right as well as on behalf of Harland & Wolff, negotiated a huge sum for the takeover of the company by J. P. Morgan's IMMC, but Ismay also secured the promise of a powerful new appointment. Two years after the takeover went through in 1904, J. Bruce Ismay took over from American Line president A. C. Griscom as chairman of the IMMC. He was now in control of the most powerful commercial shipping operation in the world.

While J. Bruce Ismay was responsible for running the IMMC, the finance behind the organization came from the legendary J. P. Morgan. John Pierpont Morgan was a man of truly formidable stature. He had been a powerful force in the American economy for more than 30 years at a time when the American economy was fast becoming a barometer for industrial, commercial and financial change the world over.

America's banker

Decisions made by Morgan reached out from his Wall Street offices to touch the lives of ordinary people not only in America but also pretty much everywhere else on the planet. He was involved in the evolving railroad business in America and in 1892 was behind the merger that created the giant General Electric company. He was one of a select few financiers who saved the U.S. government from bankruptcy in 1895 (for a tidy profit), and he bought out Andrew Carnegie to create U.S. Steel in 1901. In 1907 Morgan also bought up collapsing U.S. mining operations to save Wall Street from a similar collapse. Putting himself in the position of being America's banker, however, was a heavy burden, and the great responsibility caused Morgan huge stress, which took its toll on his health. When he was advised by his doctors to cut down on his beloved cigars, it is said he cut down to no more than 20 a day.

Around this time, Morgan's personal fortune was estimated to be worth around $20 billion—a vast sum—and maintaining it was an art at which he was quite adept. An acquaintance is said to have once asked Morgan for a loan. J.P. took the man for a stroll around New York's financial district and then said to him, "There, now that everyone has seen you keeping company with me, you'll have no trouble getting a loan anywhere you choose!"

Morgan had always been used to having or being around money. Born in 1837 in Hartford, Connecticut, he was the son of a wealthy banker. He went to college in Gottingen, Germany, and by 1857 he was working on Wall Street, establishing his own investment company in 1861 and taking over his father's banking business when his father passed away in 1890. While he was known as a great philanthropist, establishing among other public institutions the Morgan Library in New York and assembling the largest-ever private collection of works of art, much of which is now on display at New York's Metropolitan Museum, Morgan's reputation as a businessman was ferocious. Used to getting his own way and ruthless in pursuit of his ambitions, Morgan demanded respect even from the President of the United States, although he did fall foul of Theodore Roosevelt in 1902 when the government investigated one of Morgan's companies in an antitrust action. After leaving office in 1908, Roosevelt set off on a hunting trip, an African safari, the following year. When Morgan, still bitter, heard of the safari, he reportedly proposed the toast, "America expects every lion to do its duty!"

J. P. Morgan was a man well used to getting his own way, so when he decided to further his plans for a North Atlantic shipping monopoly, he demanded of J. Bruce Ismay, "Get me the finest vessels afloat." Ismay would have needed no second chance to place his beloved White Star Line so far ahead of the competition that it would take his rivals ten years to catch up.

The sketches for the new Olympic-class liners that Lord Pirrie handed to his design team became the responsibility of his brother-in-law, Alexander M. Carlisle, who was chairman of the managing directors of Harland & Wolff and ultimate head of the design department. Having started at Harland & Wolff as an apprentice, Carlisle had worked at the yard for 37 years by the time work began on the Olympic-class ships.

Although Carlisle was in overall charge of the ships' drawings and the draftsmen, he never took credit for the creation of the Olympic class ships, always maintaining that the the vessels were actually designed almost entirely by Lord Pirrie. Refining Lord Pirrie's designs, however, into the thousands of incredibly detailed engineering drawings required for the construction of a ship was the task that fell to Carlisle and the managing director of the design department, Thomas Andrews, who was also Lord Pirrie's nephew.

The talented Thomas Andrews

Andrews came from one of Ulster's most highly respected families. They had a number of business interests, including the linen industry. Thomas Andrews's father (also called Thomas) was a distinguished local politician, his uncle was a high court judge and his brother became prime minister of Northern Ireland. Born in February 1873, Thomas was educated at the Royal Belfast Academical Institute, just as both his father and Lord Pirrie had been. Like Pirrie, Thomas joined Harland & Wolff as a premium apprentice, and he threw himself into studying every aspect of the shipbuilding business. He learned the trades of the skilled workers who built the ships and attended evening classes in technical drawing, mechanics, engineering and naval architecture. On finishing his apprenticeship, Thomas worked as a repair yard manager and in 190, twelve years after joining Harland & Wolff, his talents were recognized when he became a member of the prestigious Institute of Naval Architects.

Around this time he was also appointed manager of Harland & Wolff's construction works. He was involved in the building of the White Star liners the *Adriatic*, *Baltic*, *Cedric* and *Celtic* as well as ships for the Holland-America and Red Star lines, and those who worked with him found him to be conscientious, charming and good-natured. While his colleagues might well have thought it advantageous to speak well of Thomas Andrews—he was, after all, Lord Pirrie's nephew (the son of Pirrie's sister, Eliza)—the regard and affection in which he was held seems to have been entirely genuine. Their faith in him would ultimately be borne out by the strength of character he displayed during subsequent events aboard the *Titanic*.

In June 1908, Thomas married Helen Reilly Barbour, the daughter of a former director of Harland & Wolff, and two years later their only child, Elizabeth, was born. The year 1910 also marked the retirement from Harland & Wolff of Lord Pirrie's brother-in-law, Alexander Carlisle. Carlisle has variously been described as a close confidant of Pirrie, a free thinker who could not stand the autocratic manner in which Pirrie chose to run Harland & Wolff and an eccentric and hugely talented ship designer. His direct area of responsibility on the Olympic-class ships had been the design and specification of their equipment,

Although certain specialized castings were supplied by outside companies, such as the Darlington Forge Company, which provided the brackets that housed the propeller shafts, the rudder and its mounting, Harland & Wolff also operated its own foundry. Note the foreman, or overseer, who wears a bowler hat, while the other men wear flat caps. Foremen at the yard were known as "hats."

and in conjunction with Thomas Andrews, he had recommended that there be three lifeboats at each davit–a total of 48 boats, although 64 boats were proposed at one time. This number was gradually reduced during discussions with Lord Pirrie and J. Bruce Ismay until there were only 16 standard 30-ft. (9-m) boats plus four collapsibles. The debate rages even now about whether the provision of more lifeboats on the *Titanic* would actually have helped to save more lives, given that they barely had time to launch the few they did have. But arguing points such as this–and losing–may well have contributed to Carlisle's decision to retire when he reached 40 years' service with the company. His position was filled by Thomas Andrews.

All of the aforementioned men, from William Ritchie way back in the eighteenth century right up to Thomas Andrews, played a part in the building of the *Titanic*. For some, such as Gustav Schwabe (who died in 1890 and so knew nothing of the Olympic-class liners) or J. P. Morgan, supplying the finances and dabbling in shipping was a way of increasing their personal fortunes. For others, such as Lord Pirrie, J. Bruce Ismay or Thomas Andrews, the White Star Line ships were a major part of their lives. They spent every day discussing, developing and planning the finest ocean liners in the world and they knew every plate, every bulkhead, every rivet of the ships as they were being built. But even they did not have the very real, honest, physical connection with the *Titanic* of the men who really built her, the men of Belfast who worked in the Harland & Wolff yard.

The shipyard workforce

The men who worked in the shipyards, their families and the people of Belfast were immensely proud of the ships that had been built on the River Lagan. They regarded Belfast-built ships as the best constructed in the world, and to the credit of the Belfast workers, the rest of the world tended to agree with them. The great pride taken by the people of Belfast in the city's ships grew from the way that the ships dominated the lives of so many. In the shipyards the dormant steel giants grew from nothing into massive shapes that could be seen and admired from a distance by anyone who cared to walk to the end of his street or crane his neck while standing on his own doorstep. The noise of the hammering of rivets was a constant reminder that another Belfast ship was taking shape, the sight and sound of its creation making it very much a part of the everyday life of everyone in the city.

The people most affected by the new vessels were the workers who lived with the *Titanic* and her sister ships throughout their construction every working day from 6:00 in the morning until 5:30 at night. They ate not in the company dining rooms enjoyed by the shipyard's management, but in the shadow of the ships themselves, bringing their own food for a brief breakfast break at 8:30 a.m. and another short break for lunch at 1:00 p.m. They worked up to 60 hours a week, including Saturday mornings, and would suffer stoppages from their pay if they were late for work (whatever the reason), damaged company tools or equipment, or transgressed any of the shipyard's rules and regulations. Even if workers went to watch the launch of a vessel on which they had worked, they could expect to lose a day's pay. Shipyard workers could look forward to one week's holiday in the summer, with two days off for both Christmas and Easter, all for an average wage that amounted to around £2 per week.

Senior staff or managers at the yard had things a little easier, but if they were responsible for other staff or had men reporting to them, they had to be at their posts *before* 6:00 a.m. to supervise the arrival of the workforce. Lord Pirrie, naturally, was the exception. It was his habit while in Belfast to arrive at the yard at 7:00 a.m. and spend much of the day checking on the

The Harland & Wolff shipyard in the early 1900s before it came to be dominated by the massive steel latticework of the Arrol Gantry, below which the Olympic-class liners would take shape.

progress being made in every department. Unlike the workforce, he was not expected to clock in and clock out. The Harland & Wolff workforce—15,000 men at the time the *Titanic* was being built—left their Belfast terraced houses before it was light (except for a few brief weeks during the summer months when dawn came early) and swarmed around the shipyard's entrance. There they were joined by crowds of casual laborers hoping to be taken on for the day at one of the regular early morning hiring sessions if one of the shipyard's foremen needed a few extra pairs of hands.

For many, securing regular employment at the yard meant following in their father's footsteps and learning a trade. Apprentices could be taken on as young as 14, with most apprenticeships lasting five years. The trades they could learn were many and varied. Harland & Wolff handled every aspect of a ship's construction from the laying of the keel, the framing and plating, through to the building of the engines, the installation of the equipment and fittings and the interior décor. In common with other manufacturing industries and general trades, an apprentice was expected to supply the basic tools of his trade, traditionally paid for—at least in part—by his journeyman, the qualified tradesman to whom he was apprenticed. After serving for five years, an apprentice could look forward to carrying a union card that identified him as a qualified plumber, coppersmith, riveter, plater, joiner, driller, craneman, decorator, blacksmith, ironworker, woodturner, fitter, shipwright, caulker, electrician, painter or any one of a dozen other trades.

Construction casualties

While it was a good thing to have a safe and secure job, a ship-yard was by no means a safe and secure place to work. Industrial accidents in the nineteenth and early twentieth centuries were an occupational hazard, and fatalities were common-place. In the shipbuilding industry, there was a rule of thumb that it was acceptable to incur one death among the workforce for every £100,000 spent on a project. Building the *Titanic* was to cost £1.5 million. When construction was completed, a report was submitted to a Harland & Wolff management meeting listing the casualties incurred during work on the *Titanic*. There were

254 recorded accidents: 69 in the engine works, of which 6 were listed as "severe," and 185 in the shipyard, 8 of which were fatalities. The total amount of compensation payments for the 254 accidents was £4,849 3s 5d. The company even bought two new motor cars to be used as ambulances, kept ready near the main gate to take injured workers to the hospital as quickly as possible. When work finished for the day, or at weekends when the shipyard was closed, the cars were hired out to help pay for their upkeep. Scandalous though it may seem today, eight deaths on such a huge project was well within the "acceptable" industry norm at that time. Because it has become such a legend, it is easy to forget that the *Titanic* was built almost a century ago when health and safety standards throughout the industrial world were simply not comparable with those of today. Harland & Wolff's safety standards were no worse than in any other shipyard, not that this detracts in any way from the tragedy for the families of the eight who died.

Of those eight fatalities, two were from riveting squads. This should come as no surprise considering how dangerous the riveters' job could be. Riveters worked on every part of the ship, from the dimly lit enclosed spaces inside the hull to breezy platforms over 80 ft. (24 m) high on the scaffolding or staging surrounding the ship. The entire steel structure of the *Titanic* was held together by simple rivets rather than welded joints, as welding at that time was still in its infancy. This made the riveting squads the kings of the shipyard, who earned respect from the other tradesmen for their skill and courage because, as if the circumstances of their work were not dangerous enough, the job itself was not without its hazards.

A riveting squad normally consisted of four or five men: the heater boy, the catch boy, the holder-on (in some cases the catch boy might double as a holder-on) and two riveters. The heater boy's job was to tend a coke-fired brazier or furnace in which the individual rivets were heated. He knew that when the rivet turned a certain color, he had to lift it out of the fire and get it to the riveters as quickly as possible. Plucking the rivet out of the furnace using tongs, he then rolled it down a chute to the catch boy, who would pick it up using his own tongs and run with it to where the riveters were working. There he would hand

A work party stands by a bed of sand in the foundry. Iron or steel items were made by pouring molten metal into molds carved in the sand, where the metal cooled and took on the desired basic shape. This basic casting method is still in use today.

it on to the holder-on, who would seat the rivet in the hole drilled through the two overlapping steel plates. The riveters—one left-handed and one right-handed—would then begin hammering on either side of the plates.

The riveters swung their 4-pound (1.8-kilogram) hammers in unison, striking both ends of the rivet at exactly the same instant to pound the red-hot rivet heads into the desired shape, squeezing the steel plates together. If they mistimed their initial strikes, the riveter whose hammer hit first could send a red-hot rivet shooting out of the opposite side of the plates—an extremely dangerous and costly error. The riveters, however, were masters of their craft, and the ringing of the double strikes of their hammers could be heard for miles around. After a time, the noise would make them deaf. Just like a blacksmith working at a forge, the riveters would lose a lot of sweat and generally kept a good supply of drinking water nearby to stop them from dehydrating during the course of the day.

The men had to work fast to make sure the rivet was in place while it was still hot enough to be worked, but there was another good reason for their frenetic pace—they were paid by the rivet. A tally was kept of the number of rivets seated by each squad, and at the end of the week the squad would be paid

accordingly, dividing the money among themselves as they saw fit. This meant that everyone in the team had to pull his weight and that the heater boys and catch boys were under constant pressure to keep the riveters supplied. Rushing to retrieve or deliver the next red-hot rivet was often the cause of accidents. One of the two riveting squad fatalities during the construction of the *Titanic* was 15-year-old catch boy Samuel Scott; the other was 19-year-old heater boy John Kelly. One fell from a ladder on the staging; the other fell from the slipway.

Even as the *Titanic* was launched, with the assembled dignitaries cheering as she entered the water for the first time, a tragedy was being played out on the slipway. Shipwright James Dobbin had been knocking away shoring beams beneath the hull immediately prior to the launch when some of the timbers collapsed on top of him. Seriously injured, his workmates dragged him clear and rushed him to hospital, where he later died from his injuries. Sadly, James Dobbin would not be the last of the Belfast workforce to lose his life to the *Titanic*.

The guarantee group

When a ship left the Harland & Wolff yard, completed its sea trials and was properly certified by the Board of Trade as being fit and ready to receive passengers, it was officially handed over to its owners to set sail on its maiden voyage. The ship's crew, her engineers and officers are not, at this point, as familiar with the ship as the men who built her, so it was normal practice for the shipyard to send a team of key personnel with the ship as advisors or to help deal with any teething problems. At Harland & Wolff this team was known as this guarantee group. Only the best, most proficient, most highly regarded of the shipyard workers who had built the ship could expect to be selected as part of the guarantee group. Those who were selected knew that their foremen, their managers and the company hierarchy valued their skills, trusting them to acquit themselves well, represent the company in a professional, efficient manner and conduct themselves with dignity and pride. They also knew that having been recognized as a key employee, their future with the company was assured. For all of these reasons, it was considered a great honor to be selected as part of a guarantee group.

Just over half of Harland & Wolff's workforce was required for the building of the *Olympic* and *Titanic*. Work in other parts of the complex continued, where they manufactured not only machinery and parts for their own ships but also items to order. This boiler is being loaded onto a ship for export in 1910.

The majority of those in Harland & Wolff's guarantee groups would have been incredibly excited about this wonderful opportunity. They were, after all, being rewarded for their exemplary work with a trip on an ocean liner. For many, this was the first time they had ever been on a ship that was actually doing what it was designed and built to do—sail across the ocean. This was a chance to see how well the fixtures and fittings they had installed actually performed or to learn how easy or difficult it was to operate the equipment while the ship was at sea. Practical problems that might evolve during the everyday use of a winch, a pulley or pumping equipment, the siting of a hatch, the run of a pipe or the opening of a door could be corrected or borne in mind for future reference.

The leader of the guarantee group that sailed with the *Titanic* in 1912 was, almost inevitably, Thomas Andrews. He knew every plate, beam, passage, boiler and bulkhead on the ship better than anyone else, and he was ideally placed to represent Harland & Wolff at the highest level. It was expected that when Lord Pirrie ultimately retired, Thomas Andrews would be the man to take over the company. Andrews made copious notes while aboard the *Titanic*. He carried a notebook with him in which he would jot down any ideas that came to him for improvements that might be made to the *Titanic* design when it came to building the *Gigantic*, the third of the Olympic-class liners.

Accompanying Andrews was Roderick Chisholm. A Scotsman born in Dumbarton in 1872, Chisholm had been working at Harland & Wolff in Belfast since 1892. He and his wife, Susan, had been married for 16 years and had two children, 15-year-old Alyce and 14-year-old Jimmy. Chisholm had risen to the position of chief draftsman and had worked closely with Andrews on the designs of both the *Olympic* and *Titanic*. He had actually designed the *Titanic*'s lifeboats, although the number of lifeboats carried on the ship was not his decision.

Not far from the Chisholms' home lived another senior member of the guarantee group. Anthony Frost (Artie to those who knew him well) was a 38-year-old foreman fitter who, unlike many of his contemporaries, had spent a great deal of time aboard ships at sea. He had finished his Harland & Wolff apprenticeship as a fitter in 1894 and then left the yard to spend two years at sea. Five years after he returned to the Belfast yard, Frost was promoted to leading hand fitter and in 1907, when his father, a foreman fitter, retired, Frost was given his job. He was married to Lizzie Jane, and the couple had four young children.

No survivors

Former railwayman William Parr was an assistant manager in the electrical department at Harland & Wolff, in charge of overseeing the wiring and electrical fittings on both the *Olympic* and *Titanic*. Born in Lancashire in 1882, Parr had worked as an electrician on the Lancashire and Yorkshire Railway before joining Harland & Wolff in 1910. Married with a young child, Parr was a much respected Sunday school teacher. Parr had a promising career ahead of him at Harland & Wolff, as did Robert Knight, who had worked at the yard for 21 years. Married with four children, Knight was a leading hand fitter and a conscientious worker whom most expected to be promoted to foreman before long.

Another hard worker was 18-year-old Ennis Hastings Watson. Watson was an apprentice electrician who had been studying art, electrical wiring and fitting at the Belfast Municipal Technical Institute since 1907. No one doubted that he would soon become a fully qualified electrician, especially his proud parents with whom he still lived.

Francis Parks also lived with his parents in Belfast, having been brought up in the city along with his four brothers and two sisters. Although their father was employed not at the shipyard but as an official with Belfast City Council, all five brothers worked for Harland & Wolff. Parks was an apprentice plumber when he was selected to join the *Titanic*'s guarantee group and would have had much in common with another apprentice, Alfred Cunningham. Cunningham had two sisters and three brothers. As an apprentice fitter, he worked on the guarantee group under the watchful eye of his foreman, Mr. Frost. The final member of the nine-man guarantee group was another teenage apprentice, William Campbell, an apprentice joiner who lived with his parents in Belfast.

None of the Harland & Wolff guarantee group was to survive the sinking of the *Titanic*.

Titanic's first-class reading room was situated on the port side of A Deck, the second-highest level of the ship. The white-painted wood paneling reflected the light that streamed in through the massive bay window that looked out over the promenade.

CHAPTER THREE

GRAND DESIGNS

Turning the concepts sketched out by Lord Pirrie and J. Bruce Ismay in Belgrave Square into engineering drawings from which a ship could be built was an exacting and time-consuming process, basically because the detail of the designs changed many times. The three new Olympic-class ships were visualised by Pirrie and Ismay as being virtually identical, but it quickly became clear that, for entirely practical reasons, only two could be built initially. Attempting to build the world's three largest ships simultaneously at Harland & Wolff's yard would have been almost an impossibility.

The *Olympic* and *Titanic* were to be produced first. They were designed using almost identical drawings and general plans, although changes during the design and construction meant that some relatively minor differences developed between the *Olympic* and *Titanic*. Nevertheless, they were still very much recognizable as sister ships. Pirrie and Ismay originally envisaged them as being around 100 ft. (30 m) longer than the Cunard liners *Lusitania* and *Mauretania.* They saw their new ships as having four masts and three funnels but soon revised this to two masts and four funnels. The popular conception was that the number of funnels equated directly to the power and majesty of the vessel; since the *Lusitania* and *Mauretania* had four funnels, then the Olympic-class ships also had to have four. For all practical purposes, however, venting the smoke from the *Olympic*'s or *Titanic*'s boilers would require only three funnels, the fourth funnel being little more than a showpiece used only for ventilation. From the tops of these funnels, which stood over 60 ft. (18 m.) above the boat deck, down through the ship's superstructure to the bottom of the keel would be a towering 175 ft. (53 m).

Once the funnel issue was resolved, attention could be focused on the hull dimensions. Constructing a ship 100 ft. (30 m) longer than the Cunarders was a daunting undertaking. The Tyne-built *Mauretania* outstretched her Clyde-built sister ship to achieve a length of about 790 ft. (240 m). The plans drawn up for the *Olympic* and *Titanic* showed them each to be 882 ft. 9 in. (269 m) in length, although in many specification lists the *Olympic*'s length is often rounded up to 883 ft. (269.1 m). The *Titanic* was actually undersized when

advertised on White Star Line posters as being 882 ft. 6 in. (268.9 m), and to add to the confusion, the *Titanic* is regularly quoted as being 4 in. (10 cm) longer than the *Olympic*.

Arguments over those few inches will doubtless continue to wash back and forth forever, but the fact remains that when she entered service, the *Olympic* fulfilled the dream of Lord Pirrie and J. Bruce Ismay. She was the largest ship in the world and was to remain so until the *Titanic* was handed over by Harland & Wolff to the White Star Line. The *Olympic*'s gross tonnage was 45,324, the *Titanic*'s 46,428, making the *Titanic* indisputably the world's largest ship at that time. Design details made all the difference to the *Titanic*'s tonnage, but the general look of the ships was still the same—these were, after all, the "Olympic-class" sister ships. Here, of course, it makes most sense to concentrate on the design and layout of the *Titanic*.

The deck plan

The plans drawn up for the *Titanic* showed nine decks, ten including the lowest platform, known as the Tank Top. For ease of identification by future passengers, the seven decks with passenger accommodations were referred to by letters of the alphabet, from the second-highest deck, the Promenade Deck (A), to the Lower Deck (G). Above the Promenade Deck was the Boat Deck and below the Lower Deck (it wasn't actually the lowest) were the Orlop Deck and then the Tank Top.

The Tank Top was the real basement of the ship. Moving aft, the cargo holds and reserve coal holds at the bow gave way to No. 6 boiler room, which housed four of the ship's 29 enormous boilers. Each of these boilers was like a gigantic drum, 15 ft. 9 in. (5 m) in diameter with three furnaces at either end (they were known as "double-ended" boilers), heating the water in the boiler to provide steam for the engines. At either end of No 6 boiler room were its cavernous coal bunkers, built as closely as possible to the furnaces to make the backbreaking job of shoveling coal into the hungry furnaces a little easier. Not that this arrangement was made out of compassion for the well-being of the stokers—speed and efficiency in stoking the furnaces was of primary importance.

Aft of No. 6 boiler room was, unsurprisingly, No. 5 boiler

room. The ship's hull at this point was reaching its widest, the width (or beam) of the *Titanic* a mighty 92 ft. 6 in. (28.2 m). This was over 4 ft. (1.2 m) wider than the *Mauretania*. Having more width with which to play, No. 5 boiler room could take an extra boiler and five were fitted here side by side, with the coal bunkers to feed their furnaces fore and aft of the boilers, just as in boiler room No. 6. The smoke from the furnaces of boiler rooms 6 and 5 was carried up through chimney flues that passed through every deck to disperse via the foremost funnel.

Boiler rooms No. 4 and No. 3 were laid out in a similar fashion to No. 5, with five boilers and the smoke from their furnaces venting through the second funnel, while boiler rooms No. 2 and No. 1 fed their furnace smoke out through the third fully functioning funnel. Boiler room No. 1 was a little different in that the five boilers it housed were slightly smaller at 11 ft. 9 in. (3.5 m) long and had furnaces at only one end. These "single-ended" boilers were used to provide steam for the machinery while the *Titanic* was in port, where full power was not needed for the engines. Auxiliary steam pipes from other boiler rooms could also be used to power ancillary equipment such as steam-powered winches or electrical generators. The *Titanic* had a great many electrical fittings throughout the ship, burning many times more electricity than the largest, most modern hotels of the day.

Aft of boiler room No. 1 was the main engine room, the largest space on the entire ship. The engine room soared up through the Orlop Deck, Lower Deck (G), Middle Deck (F) and Upper Deck (E), leaving the tops of the boiler rooms two decks below. At 59 ft. (18 m) long, the main engine room needed all of its length and height to accommodate the two huge reciprocating engines, each as big as a three-story house. Farther towards the stern was another engine room occupied by a smaller, yet slightly more powerful, turbine engine.

Harland & Wolff may have lacked experience with turbines and may not have had all of the technological advantages that the builders of the Cunard turbine-powered liners enjoyed courtesy of their government funding, but they were following a tried-and-tested principle of evolution rather than revolution. The turbine that was installed did not provide the sole means

of propulsion; the *Titanic* also had two huge "piston" engines, but this was a modern innovation that ran very economically on the "used" steam from the main engines. This steam otherwise would either have vented wastefully out of the funnels or have been cooled, condensed and fed back into the boilers to be reheated. While the turbine engine was not of the most advanced type, it certainly pulled, or rather pushed, its weight. In fact, it couldn't pull at all, since it could turn its central screw propeller in only one direction, providing forward propulsion. The two more traditional engines each drove their own propeller, one on the left and one on the right side of the central screw.

Beyond the turbine room was a space housing the *Titanic*'s four huge electrical generators, again producing power from steam. These were flanked by a series of fresh water storage tanks and aft of this compartment was the tapering stern of the ship where the drive shafts exited to the three gigantic propellers.

Storage and cargo space

Above the Tank Top was the Orlop Deck, and at the bow was a part-deck called the Lower Orlop Deck. In the *Titanic*'s bows, the Orlop and Lower Orlop were used for general storage and the chain locker, the space where the anchor chain was stowed when the anchors were not in use. The chain locker extended all the way up through to F Deck. Then, as far back as No 6 boiler room, there were the forward cargo holds. It was here that the Renault car bought in France by the wealthy Philadelphian Billy Carter would be stored along with other items being shipped to the United States, such as the case of machinery for the Aero Club of America or the 856 rolls of linoleum being carried for McGrachlin & Co.

The Orlop Deck forward of No. 6 boiler room was also earmarked to be used for storing baggage belonging to first- and second-class passengers. The baggage store was on the port side of the ship, while opposite, on the starboard side, was an equally large space devoted to the storage of the mail sacks, 3,364 of which would be carried on the *Titanic*'s maiden voyage. Most of the rest of the length of the Orlop

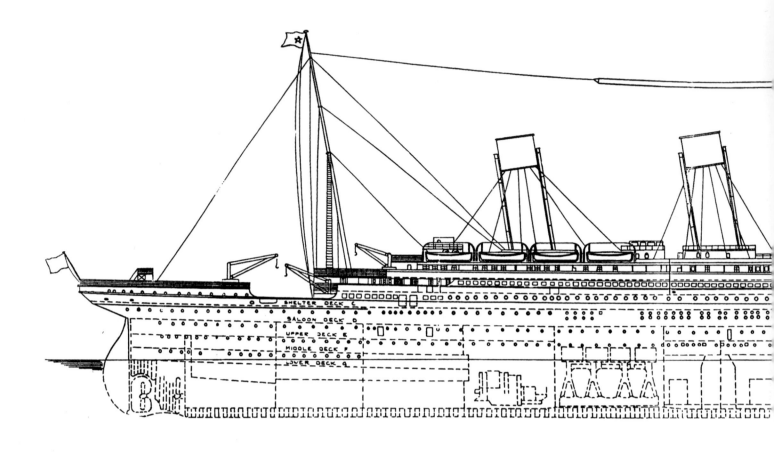

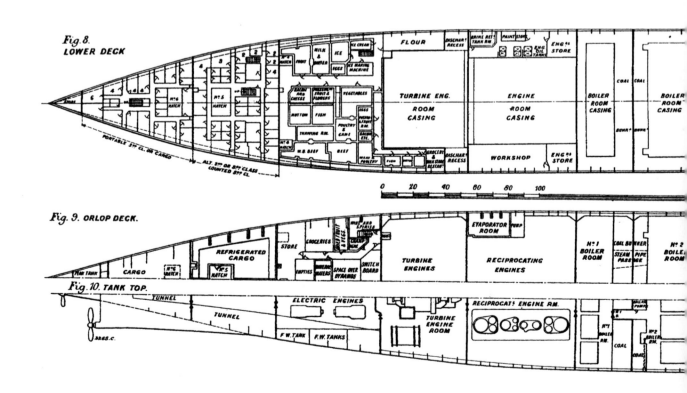

Fig. 8.
LOWER DECK

Fig. 9. ORLOP DECK.

Fig. 10. TANK TOP.

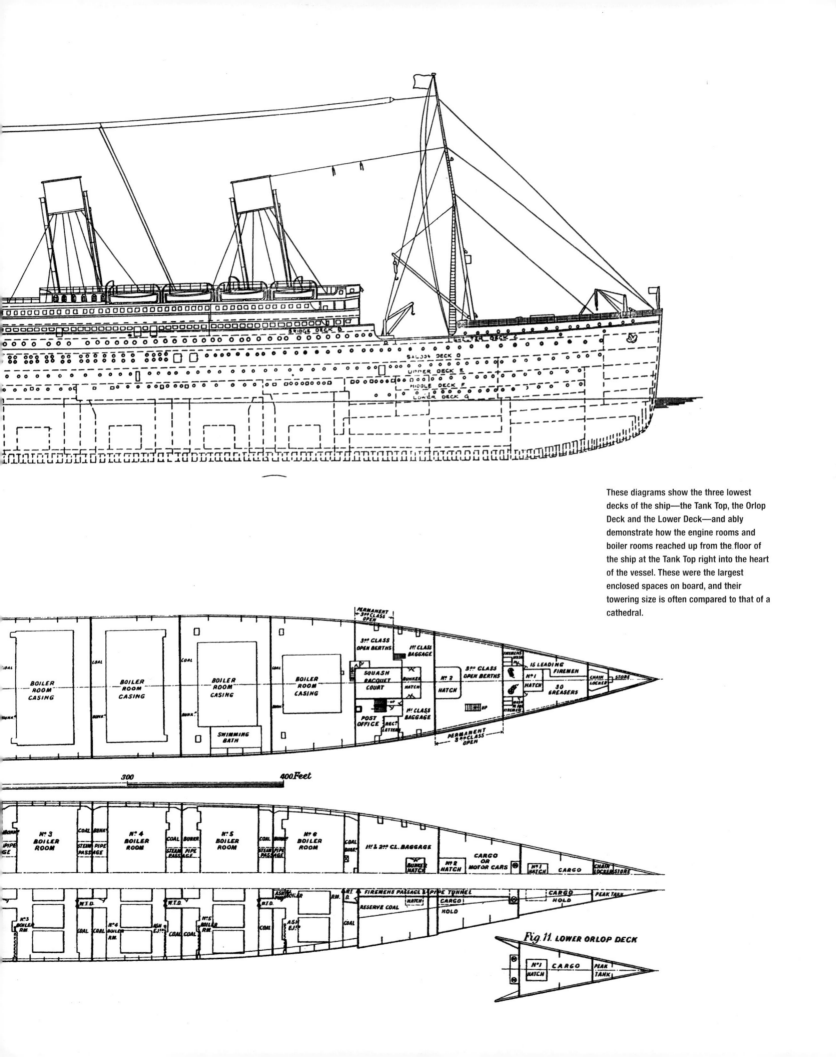

These diagrams show the three lowest decks of the ship—the Tank Top, the Orlop Deck and the Lower Deck—and ably demonstrate how the engine rooms and boiler rooms reached up from the floor of the ship at the Tank Top right into the heart of the vessel. These were the largest enclosed spaces on board, and their towering size is often compared to that of a cathedral.

Fig. 11. LOWER ORLOP DECK

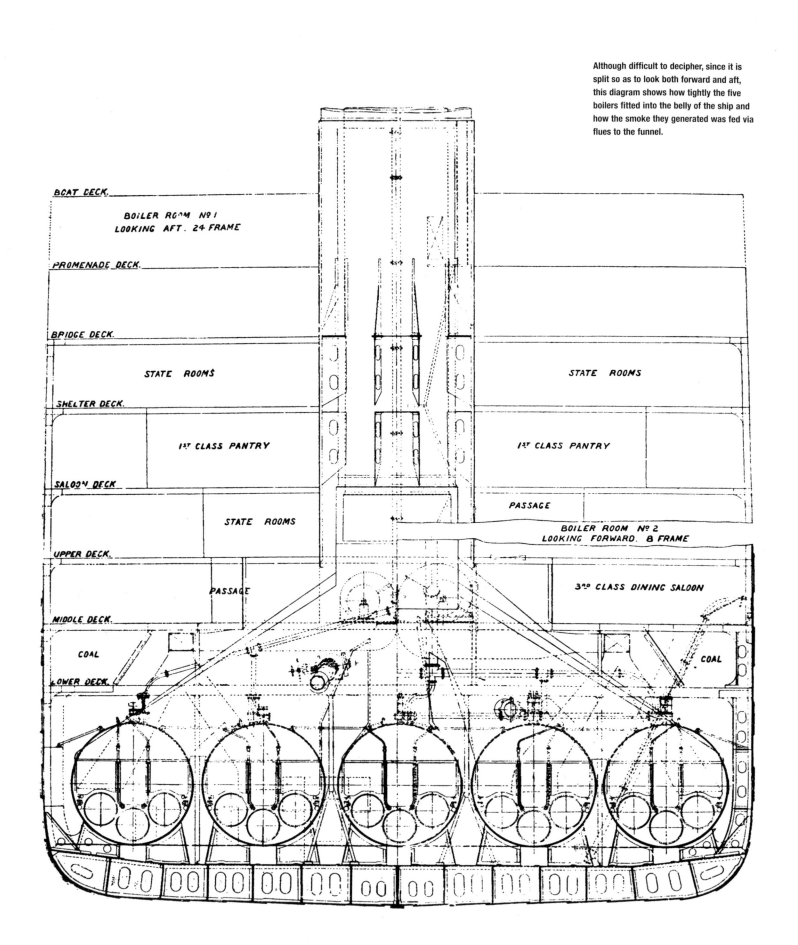

Although difficult to decipher, since it is split so as to look both forward and aft, this diagram shows how tightly the five boilers fitted into the belly of the ship and how the smoke they generated was fed via flues to the funnel.

BOAT DECK.

BOILER ROOM Nº 1
LOOKING AFT. 24 FRAME

PROMENADE DECK.

BRIDGE DECK.

STATE ROOMS

STATE ROOMS

SHELTER DECK.

1ST CLASS PANTRY

1ST CLASS PANTRY

SALOON DECK

PASSAGE

STATE ROOMS

BOILER ROOM Nº 2
LOOKING FORWARD. 8 FRAME

UPPER DECK.

PASSAGE

3RD CLASS DINING SALOON

MIDDLE DECK.

COAL

COAL

LOWER DECK.

This plan of boiler rooms 1 and 2 shows the single-ended boilers in No. 1 and the double-ended boilers in No. 2 with their flues feeding up towards the smokestack or funnel.

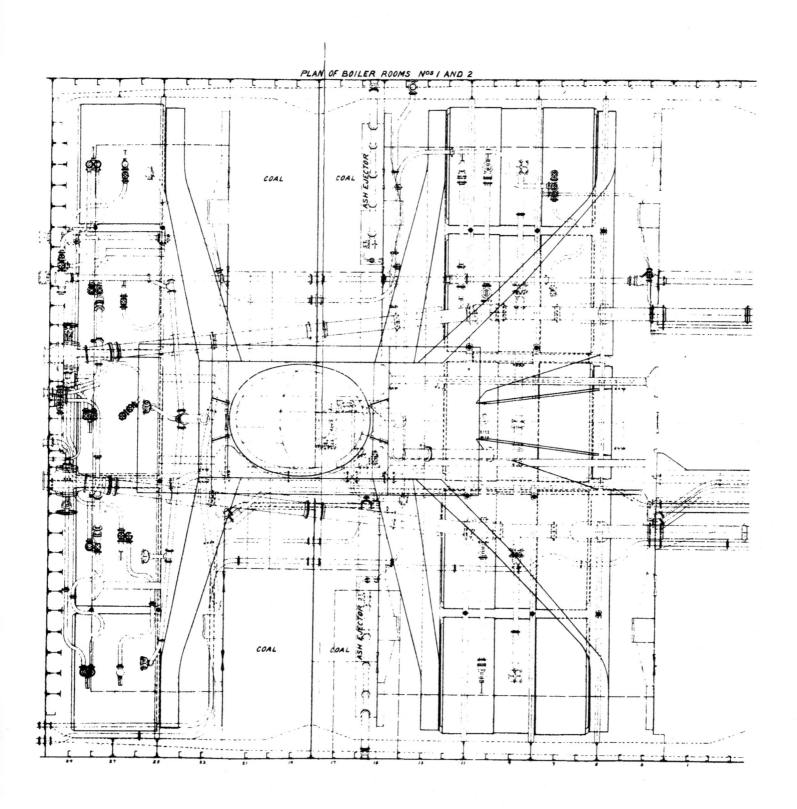

PLAN OF BOILER ROOMS Nᵒˢ I AND 2

Fig. 4. SHELTER DECK. (C)

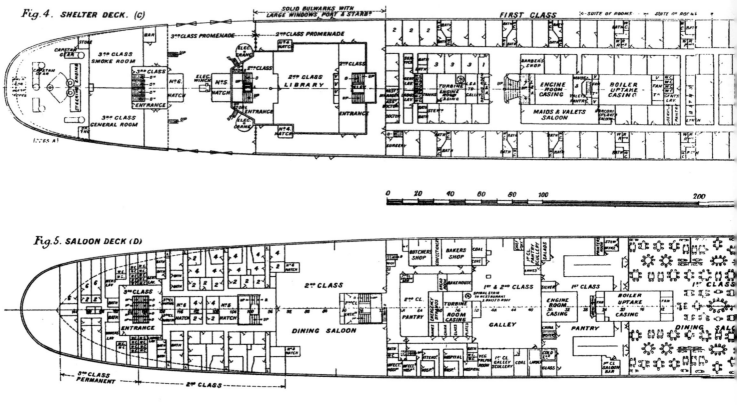

Fig. 5. SALOON DECK (D)

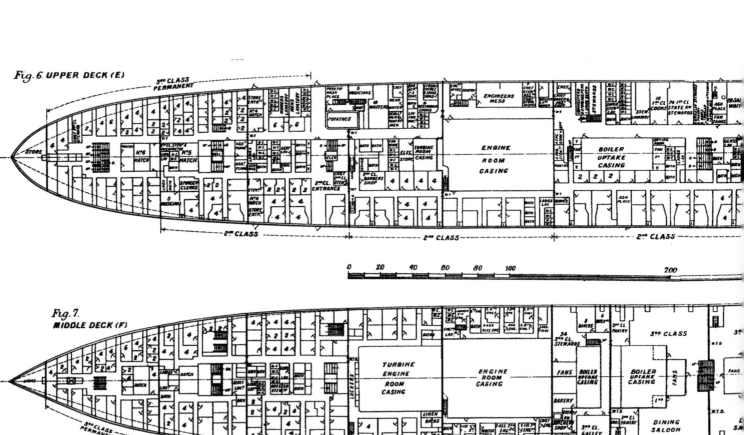

Fig. 6. UPPER DECK (E)

Fig. 7. MIDDLE DECK (F)

These plans of decks F to C show that while passenger accommodation stretched all the way down to G Deck, the first-class cabins did not begin until E Deck. Facilities for first-class passengers, of course, extended into the lower decks, with the swimming, bath and steam room on F Deck and the squash court all the way down on G Deck.

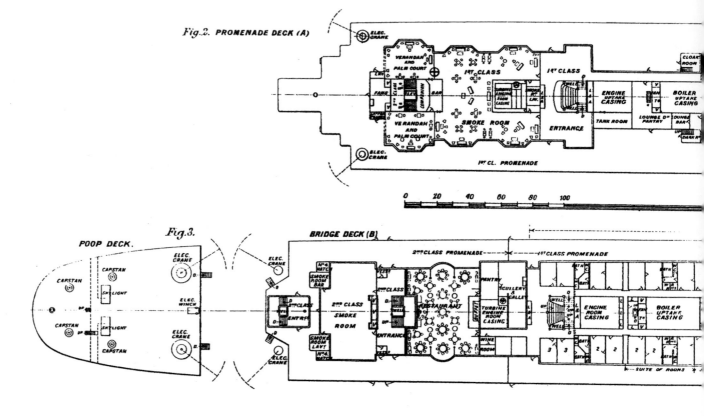

Fig.2. PROMENADE DECK (A)

ELEC. CRANE

VERANDAH AND PALM COURT

1ST CLASS

1ST CLASS

ENGINE UPTAKE CASING

BOILER UPTAKE CASING

CLOAK ROOM

1ST CLASS LOUNGE

BAR

ENGINE ROOM CASING

ENTRANCE

TANK ROOM

LOUNGE PANTRY

LOUNGE BAR

VERANDAH AND PALM COURT

SMOKE ROOM

ELEC. CRANE

1ST CL. PROMENADE

0   20   40   60   80   100

Fig.3.

POOP DECK.

ELEC. CRANE

CAPSTAN

CAPSTAN

SKYLIGHT

SKYLIGHT

CAPSTAN

ELEC. CRANE

ELEC. WINCH

ELEC. CRANE

ELEC. CRANE

BRIDGE DECK (B)

2ND CLASS PROMENADE

1ST CLASS PROMENADE

No 4 HATCH

SMOKE ROOM BAR

2ND CLASS ENTR'E

2ND CLASS SMOKE ROOM

SMOKE ROOM LAVT.

No 4 HATCH

2ND CLASS

PANTRY

SCULLERY & GALLEY

RESTAURANT

ENTRANCE

WINE ROOM

TURBINE ENGINE ROOM CASING

ENGINE ROOM CASING

BOILER UPTAKE CASING

SUITE OF ROOMS

THE WHITE STAR LINERS

CONSTRUCTED BY MESSRS. HARLAND AND WOLFF,

The plans of the three uppermost decks show how much space was allocated to the most expensive staterooms and to the first-class public areas, as well as how tragically few lifeboats were carried on the *Titanic*.

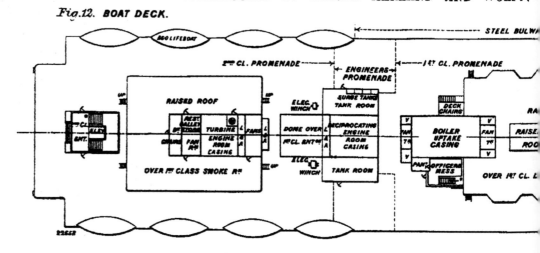

Fig.12. BOAT DECK.

360 LIFEBOAT

STEEL BULWA

2ND CL. PROMENADE

ENGINEERS PROMENADE

1ST CL. PROMENADE

1ST CL. ENT.

RAISED ROOF

REST VALLEY TORE

TURBINE ENGINE ROOM CASING

FAN RM

OVER 1ST CLASS SMOKE RM

ELEC. WINCH

SURGE TANK TANK ROOM

DOME OVER

1ST CL. ENT.

RECIPROCATING ENGINE ROOM CASING

ELEC. WINCH

TANK ROOM

DECK CHAIRS

BOILER UPTAKE CASING

FAN

OFFICERS MESS

OVER 1ST CL.

FAN

RA

RAISE

ROO

FIG. 12. TH

0   20   40   60   80   100

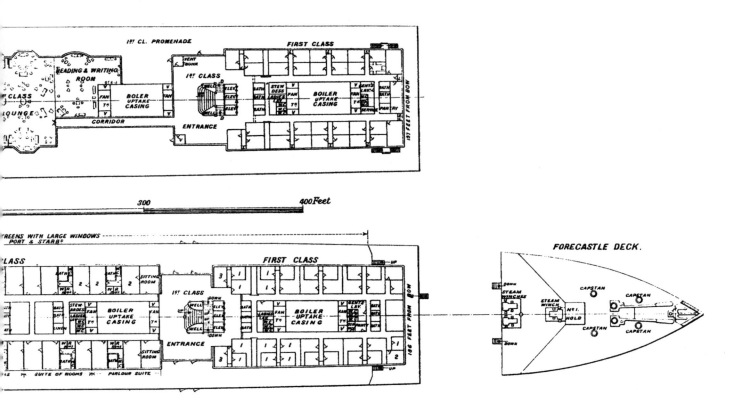

First diagram labels:
1ST CL. PROMENADE — FIRST CLASS — READING & WRITING ROOM — BOILER UPTAKE CASING — 1ST CLASS — BOILER UPTAKE CASING — CORRIDOR — ENTRANCE — CLASS — LOUNGE — VENT TRUNK — FAN — STEW DESS LADIES — GENTS LAV. — BATH — SERVICE PANTRY — 197 FEET FROM BOW

300   400 Feet

SCREENS WITH LARGE WINDOWS PORT & STARB⁰ — FIRST CLASS — CLASS — SITTING ROOM — 1ST CLASS WELL — BOILER UPTAKE CASING — ELEV — BOILER UPTAKE CASING — ENTRANCE — STEW ARDESS LADIES LAV — LINEN — SITTING ROOM — SUITE OF ROOMS — PARLOUR SUITE — 186 FEET FROM BOW

FORECASTLE DECK.

DOWN — STEAM WINCHES — STEAM WINCH — CAPSTAN — CAPSTAN — N° 1. HOLD — CAPSTAN — CAPSTAN — DOWN

YMPIC" AND "TITANIC."

ED, SHIPBUILDERS AND ENGINEERS, BELFAST.

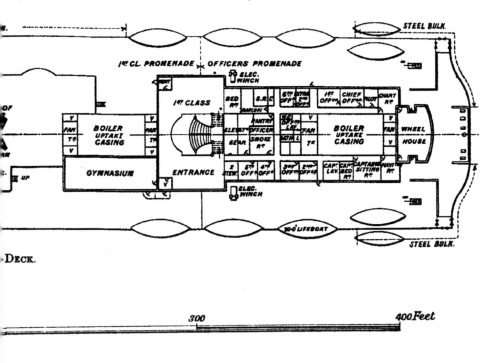

STEEL BULK.

1ST CL. PROMENADE — OFFICERS PROMENADE — ELEC. WINCH — 1ST CLASS — BED R° — S.R° — 6TH EXTRA OFF — 1ST OFF — CHIEF OFF — PILOT — CHART R° — BOILER UPTAKE CASING — FAN — ELEVAT — PANTRY — 5TH OFFICER — 2ND OFF — MARCONI — GEAR — SMOKE R° — BTH W.C — BOILER UPTAKE CASING — FAN — WHEEL HOUSE — GYMNASIUM — ENTRANCE — 2 STEW — 5TH OFF — 4TH OFF — 3RD OFF — 2ND OFF — CAP. OFF — CAP. LAV. — CAPTAINS BED R° — CAPTAINS SITTING R° — NAVI R° — ELEC. WINCH — 30-0 LIFEBOAT — STEEL BULK.

DECK.

300   400 Feet

Deck, the vast belly of the ship, was taken up by boiler spaces, and engine and turbine rooms, but aft of the turbine, above the electrical generators, was another useful space. There was a switchboard platform where the electricity supply was routed to the various circuits around the ship and a number of storage spaces. A bulk store, steward's workstore and mineral water store were fitted in along with storerooms for groceries, fruit and vegetables, and wines and spirits. Next door to the wines and spirits store was a separate room solely for champagne, which some of the *Titanic's* first-class passengers would drink with every course during dinner. On the starboard side and to the rear of these storage areas were special refrigerator rooms for keeping perishable cargo, with an additional standard-cargo hold right at the stern of the Orlop Deck.

Above the Orlop Deck on G Deck (Lower Deck), the bow space was used as a storage locker and the chain locker extended up from the deck below. Moving aft were the first of the *Titanic's* berths, a port dormitory where 15 leading firemen slept and a starboard one housing 30 greasers. Each of the dormitories had its own washroom and immediately aft of these crew quarters was the first passenger accommodation. Situated above the main forward cargo hold was a large, full-width open dormitory for third-class passengers. Additional first-class baggage holds separated these passenger berths from a smaller third-class dormitory area on the port side and the ship's post office on the starboard side. Above the mail storage area, with its own secure storage for registered letters (200 sacks of which were to travel with the *Titanic),* was where the five mail clerks would work, sorting the letters, parcels and packages while the ship was en route to New York.

Between the smaller port dormitory and the post office was the *Titanic's* squash court. This novel facility was 30 ft. (9 m) long, 20 ft. (6 m) wide and reached all the way up into F deck. Use of the squash court was restricted to first-class passengers. For those proficient enough to tackle a contest, the court could be booked at the enquiry office on C Deck, at a cost of two shillings per half hour. For those who required a few pointers, a resident squash professional, Mr. Frederick Wright, was on hand to provide instruction.

This forward area of G Deck then gave way to the bunkers, boilers and engine spaces that now included the engineers' stores, paint stores and workshops. Farther astern, aft of the turbine room, a cluster of food-storage spaces for everything from beef, poultry, game and mutton to bacon, cheese, butter and ice cream held the bulk of the *Titanic's* provisions.

Passenger accommodation

The aft section of G Deck housed the first of the passenger cabins—two- or four-berth cabins for second-class passengers with one three-berther on both the port and starboard sides. These most basic second-class cabins were remarkably well appointed. Most had mahogany furniture, even though this consisted of upper and lower bunks, with curtains to provide a modicum of privacy for the occupants. They also had sofa beds that could be used as seating during the day, linoleum floor coverings rather than a bare, painted steel deck, electric lights,

wood-paneled walls and mahogany washstands. The overall finish was to a standard that made the *Titanic*'s second-class berths the equal of the majority of the White Star Line's rivals' first-class cabins. This second-class accommodation gave way to third-class two-, four- or six-berth cabins at the ship's stern. The small two-berth cabins had foldaway bunks to give more living space during the day, but even though these cabins provided the most spartan accommodation, they still had floor coverings, electric lights and, in most cases, a wash basin with running water. This was pure luxury compared with most other "immigrant" ships of the period and a far better bedroom than many of the third-class passengers would have been used to at home!

Nevertheless, these cabins would be the least desirable on the ship because they were situated in one of the areas of the ship that was likely to suffer most from pitching and swaying as she plowed across the Atlantic. The bow and stern of a ship

are subjected to more vertical movement as the vessel rides through the waves than the central section. The effect is rather like a see-saw, though not quite so extreme, with the ship "pivoting" on the midsection. The movement is generally felt most in the bow, where it is compounded by the crashing of waves—although in the lower stern decks passengers could also suffer from vibration caused by the propellers. That is why the lower-ranking crew members' quarters and the passengers who had bought the cheapest fares were housed in the bow or stern.

The third-class cabins at the stern were also envisaged as being "portable" because the walls could be moved to make them larger or smaller as required. Not only could the layout of the cabins be reconfigured, but the cabins could be stripped out altogether to convert the area into a cargo space. This was to make the return journey from New York to Southampton more profitable, as there were never likely to be as many

Far left: This illustration is an artist's impression of a second-class cabin aboard the *Titanic*, produced for publicity purposes prior to the completion of the ship.

Left: The swimming bath was reserved for first-class passengers, with ladies and gentlemen being allocated different periods during the day when they could swim. This photograph shows the *Olympic*'s pool, although it is identical to the one aboard the *Titanic*.

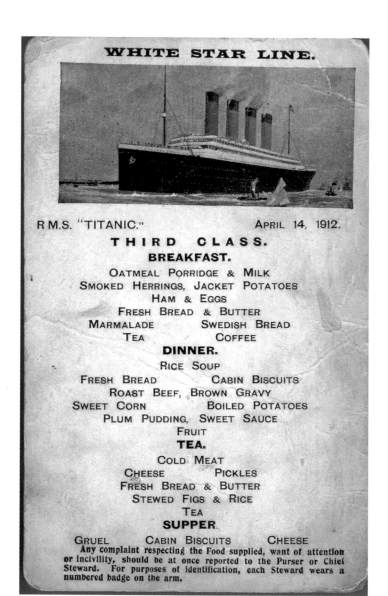

WHITE STAR LINE.

R.M.S. "TITANIC." APRIL 14, 1912.

THIRD CLASS.

BREAKFAST.

OATMEAL PORRIDGE & MILK
SMOKED HERRINGS, JACKET POTATOES
HAM & EGGS
FRESH BREAD & BUTTER
MARMALADE   SWEDISH BREAD
TEA   COFFEE

DINNER.

RICE SOUP
FRESH BREAD   CABIN BISCUITS
ROAST BEEF, BROWN GRAVY
SWEET CORN   BOILED POTATOES
PLUM PUDDING, SWEET SAUCE
FRUIT

TEA.

COLD MEAT
CHEESE   PICKLES
FRESH BREAD & BUTTER
STEWED FIGS & RICE
TEA

SUPPER.

GRUEL   CABIN BISCUITS   CHEESE

Any complaint respecting the Food supplied, want of attention or incivility, should be at once reported to the Purser or Chief Steward. For purposes of identification, each Steward wears a numbered badge on the arm.

R.M.S. "TITANIC"

APRIL 14, 1912.

LUNCHEON.

CONSOMMÉ FERMIER   COCKIE LEEKIE
FILLETS OF BRILL
EGG À L'ARGENTEUIL
CHICKEN À LA MARYLAND
CORNED BEEF, VEGETABLES, DUMPLINGS

FROM THE GRILL.

GRILLED MUTTON CHOPS
MASHED, FRIED & BAKED JACKET POTATOES

CUSTARD PUDDING
APPLE MERINGUE   PASTRY

BUFFET.

SALMON MAYONNAISE   POTTED SHRIMPS
NORWEGIAN ANCHOVIES   SOUSED HERRINGS
PLAIN & SMOKED SARDINES
ROAST BEEF
ROUND OF SPICED BEEF
VEAL & HAM PIE
VIRGINIA & CUMBERLAND HAM
BOLOGNA SAUSAGE   BRAWN
GALANTINE OF CHICKEN
CORNED OX TONGUE
LETTUCE   BEETROOT   TOMATOES

CHEESE.

CHESHIRE, STILTON, GORGONZOLA, EDAM,
CAMEMBERT, ROQUEFORT, ST. IVEL.
CHEDDAR

Iced draught Munich Lager Beer 3d. & 6d. a Tankard.

Above left: The third-class menu for all meals on April 14, 1912. The choices for the full day take up fewer lines than those for lunch alone in first class (right). For many third-class passengers, however, these could be the best meals they had ever eaten. For many, these would also be their last.

passengers paying lower fares (mostly the "immigrant trade") traveling eastbound across the Atlantic. There would always be some people, of course, who either found America not to be the land of opportunity of which they had dreamed or who had made enough money to be able to return home to their families. These few thousand passengers each year, however, would not fill all of the berths on a ship such as the *Titanic* on every return trip. There was far more demand for goods produced or manufactured in the United States to be transported back to Europe, and these third-class cabins above the rear cargo hold could themselves be turned into a valuable cargo space.

Climbing up to F Deck, also known as the Middle Deck, the bow space was once more utilized in the traditional manner for storage with the chain locker immediately behind this space and, beyond that, following a familiar pattern, crew accommodation. These were to be the quarters of the ship's firemen and a handful of leading greasers. The forward section behind the crew facilities was taken up by over 70 third-class cabins, ranging in size from two to ten berths. Far more of the deck space could now be devoted to passenger accommodation, as the intrusion from the boiler rooms below was greatly reduced because the flues converged to be channeled upwards toward their allotted funnels. A larger intrusion from below was caused by the height of the squash court and its gallery for spectators.

On the starboard side of the squash court, surrounded by third-class cabins, were the mail clerks' berths, directly above the post office. Although space on the plans was allocated for only two clerks, the *Titanic* actually had five. These men were not employees of the White Star Line; they worked for the sea post office and were based in Southampton and New York. There had been some complaints from the postal workers on the *Olympic* about the siting of their berths because third-class passengers in the surrounding cabins kept them awake singing and partying into the wee hours. The passengers could hardly be blamed—they were, after all, on a cruise bound for a new life in America and entitled to celebrate. The mail clerks, however, had a full day's work ahead of them. During the voyage on the *Titanic*, this would mean sorting around 400,000 items of mail

from the 1,758 sacks loaded at Southampton, 1,142 loaded at Cherbourg and 194 at Queenstown. They also had to deal with the postcards and letters mailed by the passengers while the ship was under way. Three of the mail clerks were American—William Gwinn, John March and Oscar Woody—while the others, John Smith and James Williamson, were British. On the evening of April 14, 1912, far out in the Atlantic, they were unlikely to be disturbed by the passengers' revelry because they were celebrating Oscar Woody's forty-fourth birthday.

The swimming pool

Moving aft from the passenger cabins, there were linen storage and drying rooms on the port side, while on the starboard side nestled one of the *Titanic*'s most notable innovations—the swimming pool. The *Olympic* and *Titanic* were among the first ships ever to boast a swimming pool, but this was not the kind of makeshift, canvas-lined cargo hold some ships might have called a swimming pool. The Titanic's swimming pool was indoors, bright and modern, flanked on one side by two shower stalls and a row of changing cubicles. On the other side, daylight flooded in through an array of portholes. The pool, known as the swimming bath, was fully tiled and filled with heated salt water to a depth of 6 ft. (1.8 m). The final version on the finished ship was free for the use of male first-class passengers from 6:00 a.m. to 9:00 a.m. Thereafter, tickets could be purchased from the enquiry office on C Deck for one dollar or four shillings. Ladies had exclusive use of the pool from 10:00 a.m. to 1:00 p.m., and gentlemen could swim from 2.00 p.m. to 6.00 p.m. As with the squash court, use of the swimming bath was restricted to first-class passengers whatever the time of day.

The swimming pool was not the only facility available on F Deck for the pampering of first-class passengers. Aft of the swimming bath were a separate steam room, hot room, temperate room, cooling room and shampoo room. This was the equivalent of what we would today call a leisure suite; on the *Titanic* it was called the Turkish bath. The Turkish bath operated on the same principle as the swimming bath with tickets available from the enquiry office, ladies from 10:00 a.m.

until 1:00 p.m. and gentlemen from 2:00 p.m. until 6:00 p.m. The most incredible part of the Turkish bath was undoubtedly the cooling room, which was decorated in Arabian style. It was furnished with low loungers, canvas darkwood deck chairs and side tables where overheated refugees from the steam room or hot room could relax with a refreshing glass of cold water from the marble drinking fountain. Looking around, they could admire the intricate fretwork on what was described as "an elaborately carved Cairo curtain through which the light fitfully reveals something of the grandeur of the mysterious East." In fact, the screens were disguising the rather less mysterious portholes.

The tiles covering the walls of this room above the teak dado rail were equally impressive. They were arranged in panels of blue and green, while on the ceiling the gilt-faced beams and cornices were complemented by bronze Arab lamps. The normal pillars, or stanchions, of the ship were suitably concealed behind carved teak casings, matching the teak paneling on the walls below the dado rail, and the floor was covered with a geometrically patterned linoleum. Here you could forget that you were on board a ship completely.

Third-class meals

Opposite the Turkish bath area on the port side, beyond where the boiler-room flues rose through the deck, were storage rooms and dormitory berths for more than 40 third-class stewards and 15 cooks. Aft of this section was the first of the passengers' public areas to stretch the full width of the ship, although again, with the rising flues intruding. This was the third-class dining saloon, 100 ft. (30 m) long and formed by two rooms divided across the width of the ship by a bulkhead, but intended to be laid out uniformly. On the *Titanic* this would ultimately mean white enamel-painted walls and long tables laid for at least eight, where the diners would eat breakfast, lunch (referred to as dinner in third class), dinner (called tea and served early evening) and a late supper.

The third-class passengers had their meals included in the price of their ticket but still ate handsomely. Breakfast might consist of porridge with milk, kippers or beefsteak and onions, baked potatoes, fresh bread and butter, marmalade, tea or

coffee. Dinner might start with soup, followed by corned beef and cabbage with potatoes, then a fruit pudding such as peaches and rice. There would usually be a fish alternative to the meat course, and kosher meat could be supplied for Jewish passengers. For tea there would be some kind of cooked course followed by cheese and pickles, then buns or bread and jam. Cheese, cabin biscuits and tea or coffee were available at dinner or teatime and also comprised the main elements of the late supper. This was a lot more food than many third-class passengers would ever have eaten before in one day. Up to 470 passengers could be served in the third-class dining saloon, and there were three sittings for each meal.

Astern of the third-class dining saloon were the third-class pantries, the galleys and crew accommodation for butchers, bakers and stewards. Berths and facilities for the engineering crew filled the port and starboard sides of the next section of F Deck, separated by the higher part of the engine room. Beyond that, two- and four-berth second-class cabins were planned with two-, four-, five- and six-berth third-class cabins occupying the sternmost part of the deck. Although most cabins were intended to have some form of washing facility, there were no toilets in any of the cabins on either F or G Decks. In fact, there were no passenger toilet facilities planned for G Deck at all. Those in the stern cabins on G Deck would have to use the toilets located upstairs on F Deck, and those in the bow cabins on G and F decks would have to make use of the facilities even farther upstairs on E Deck.

In the very bow on E Deck (the Upper Deck), there was a store and crew dormitories for the ship's trimmers, who handled the coal for the furnaces. There were bunks for more than 70 trimmers here as well as an additional seamen's dormitory, crew facilities, washrooms and toilets for third-class passengers and a scattering of third-class cabins. Here, too, was the cabin of the master-at-arms, the man responsible for maintaining discipline aboard ship. The midsection of the ship on the starboard side was devoted to crew's quarters for everyone from the carpenters and the quartermaster to the cooks, chefs, plate washers and bakers. Most of the accommodation here, however, was occupied by an army of

Francis Browne was a 32-year-old student priest who traveled first class from Southampton aboard the *Titanic*, disembarking at Queenstown. He took many photographs during his short voyage, including this one of the dressing table in his cabin.

waiters, stewards and assistant stewards. The passage outside their quarters was a constant bustle of to-ing and fro-ing as these crew members came on or off duty—so much so that this gangway became known as "Scotland Road," named after a busy working-class area of Liverpool, the *Titanic*'s home port.

Park Lane

The reason that all of these stewards and stewardesses were housed in the starboard midsection of E Deck was because directly opposite, on the port side beyond the ever decreasing intrusion of the boiler flues, were the first of the first-class cabins. For those first-class passengers who had not brought their own servants with them, it was imperative that their steward be readily available. Another, narrower passageway ran past these first-class cabins. It was nicknamed "Park Lane."

These cabins were the most basic of the first-class accommodation. They were originally intended to sleep two, three or four, and had brass "cot" beds with a low guardrail. This ran from the head partway down the side of the bed to stop those in a deep sleep from rolling out of bed when the ship moved around in heavy seas. These guards, a common feature on ships' bunks, were also used on the beds in the more expensive first-class cabins, where they would become one of the few reminders that the room was actually a cabin aboard ship rather than a luxury hotel room. The E Deck cabins had wood paneling on the walls, concealing the ship's steel superstructure and pipework—the paneling was painted and hung with reproductions of works of art. The cabins were equipped with electric lighting and, of course, an electric bell-push to summon a steward. The passengers who would occupy these cabins would pay £23 for their one-way ticket across the Atlantic. The ticket price did not include meals.

Aft of the first-class cabins on the starboard side were two- and four-berth second-class cabins and one larger cabin with berths allotted for five ship's musicians. In the end, more berths would have to have been found, since the *Titanic* sailed with eight musicians. The violinist Wallace Hartley, who had been head-hunted from Cunard's *Mauretania*, was the band leader when the quartet played in the first-class dining room. The remaining trio—a violinist, cellist and pianist—would play alternately in the second-class dining room or the first-class reception room outside the à la carte restaurant on B Deck. Other crew members, such as the purser's clerks, were also allocated berths in second class on E Deck, and space was also given over to the second-class barbershop. There were two fully equipped barbershops on board, one in second and one in first class, each boasting the most modern appliances—even hair dryers—and where gentlemen could enjoy a haircut or a luxurious shave seated in a proper barber's chair. The barbershops also sold trinkets, souvenirs and postcards.

Left: A first-class suite, spacious enough easily to accommodate a table, couch and several chairs in the bedroom as well as the double bunk.

Above left: Another first-class suite in a different style, with the door open to show the private drawing room adjoining.

Above right: This first-class suite boasts a curtained four-poster–style double bunk.

Opposite the second-class cabins, the starboard side of E deck consisted mainly of stores and crew quarters, while the after section was devoted to third-class cabins. Although it might seem strange to have sections of first-, second- and third-class cabins running concurrently on the same deck, the passengers were carefully segregated. It would not do to have those paying first-class fares mixing with those in third class, even though E Deck was the first deck where it was possible to walk all the way from the bow to the stern of the ship. To allow passengers to move between decks without straying into the wrong areas, there were separate third-, second- and first-class stairways. There were also separate elevators for first and second class (none for third). These were another of the *Titanic*'s unique innovations, intended to give her even more of the feel of a luxury hotel. Built and installed by the Otis elevator

company, there were three elevators, each with an attendant, designed to be incorporated into the main first-class stairway and running from E Deck up to A (the Promenade) Deck. The single second-class elevator was built into the main second-class stairway in the after part of the midship section and ran from F Deck all the way up to the Boat Deck. Like the three first-class elevators, there were stops on each deck.

Segregation was not only to be applied between the different classes of passenger but also between the sexes in third class. Men and women traveling alone or unmarried were separated, the male berths in the bow of the third-class sections and the female berths in the stern sections. Obviously, it was expected that passengers traveling alone in first or second class would behave with the utmost of decorum, while it was thought best not to tempt the third-class travelers to turn the *Titanic* into the *Love Boat*.

One area where the ladies and gentlemen traveling third class could mix freely was the third-class open space on D Deck, the Saloon Deck. Designed as a rather bland and spartan area behind the store and crew quarters in the bow of D Deck, the open space was punctuated by the hatch that

descended all the way down to the reserve coal bunkers on the Tank Top level and No. 2 hatch, one of the ship's main cargo hatches. An obvious alternative use for the third-class open space was as an auxiliary cargo hold. Beyond this space, and distinctly separate from it, on both the port and starboard sides, were more first-class cabins with stewards' quarters tucked away here and there among the first-class washrooms. The passageways here led on to the first-class entrances on both the port and starboard sides. At the dockside or in the harbor when passengers were embarking, the doors through the hull into these halls would be the lowest level at which first-class passengers were able to board the ship. At sea the entrance halls were to form a link between the first-class cabin passageways and the first-class reception area.

In the reception area was the bottom of the magnificent grand staircase. The delicate, swirling wrought-iron work and intricate marquetry on the woodwork of the balustrades, along with the finely carved newel posts and their highly decorative carved caps, made this sweeping staircase a delight to behold from this lowest level right up to the top of the stairs on the Boat Deck. The walls were clad in oak paneling, and the stairwell was crowned with an ornate dome of opaque glass panels supported by a lattice of iron framing.

The reception area itself was elegantly furnished with comfortably upholstered sofas, a scattering of tables, cane chairs and dark carpeting covering a floor that stretched the full width of the vessel. The overall theme of the room was intended to be Jacobean, with bronze wall lights casting

At over 100ft. in length, the dining saloon was the largest room afloat. Around the walls were alcoves where tables were arranged to provide diners with some privacy, while screens could be requested for an even cozier dining experience.

The central section of the dining room was designed as a dance floor with a raised orchestra platform. At the opposite end of the dining room from the reception area was the first-class pantry, which led on to silver, china, cutlery and glass stores before you reached the galley. Food for both the first- and second-class dining rooms was prepared here on two enormous ranges that were said to be the biggest in the world. There were 19 ovens, 4 silver grills, 2 large roasters, steam ovens, steam stockpots and an array of electric gadgets for slicing, carving, peeling, mincing or whisking. There were also cold stores, a bakery, a baker's shop, a butcher's shop and coal bunkers to feed the ranges' ovens.

The final dinner

It was here that the final first-class dinner was prepared. The food on board the *Titanic* amply lived up to the ship's claim of providing everything that a top London or New York hotel could offer.

For dinner on April 14 (the last supper for so many), the first-class menu, printed within a folder which pictured Europa and Columbia above a radiant white star, offered a lavish seven-course meal. It included various hors d'oevres or oysters; a choice of two soups and a choice of seven main courses, rolling on through salad, pâté, sweets and ice cream to finish with a dessert of assorted fresh fruit and cheese.

Aft of the galley on the starboard side, and completely separate from the galley, was the ship's hospital, with its own stair access to the floors below and above.

Directly behind the galley was the second-class pantry, the facilities of which, on a smaller scale, mirrored those in the first-class pantry. This opened into the second-class dining saloon, where passengers sat at long tables in fixed, swivel chairs—a seating style found even in first class on most liners in 1912. Diners entered this room via doors from the second-class main stairway, which, with its dark, gleaming, polished oak

patterns on the white-painted wood paneling and a white plaster ceiling, where additional electric lights gave the room a very bright and airy feel. This was the area designed for first-class passengers to relax with cocktails before dinner, at which time they walked through revolving doors into the main first-class dining saloon. Again stretching the full width of the ship and running to 114 ft. (35 m) in length, this room was the largest public area on the ship. More than 550 diners could be served at any one sitting. The White Star Line described it as:

An immense room decorated in a style peculiarly English, reminiscent of early Jacobean times; but instead of the somber oak of the sixteenth and seventeenth centuries, it is painted a soft, rich white, which, with the coved and richly molded ceilings and the spacious character of the apartment, would satisfy the most aesthetic critic. The furniture is of oak designed to harmonize with its surroundings.

balustrade and matching wall panels was if not as breathtaking as the first-class grand staircase, still of a standard to grace a country house hotel. The oak paneling on the walls of the stairway was carried through into the dining room, which again stretched the width of the ship, but at 71 ft. (22 m) long could seat only 394 diners. Despite being prepared in the same galley, the food on the second-class menu was not of the same quality as that offered to first-class diners; but while it was simpler fare, it would still include six courses.

The aft exit from the second-class dining room led out onto the second of the second-class stairways and a range of second-class cabins beyond which, at the stern of D Deck, were the third-class stairway and additional third-class cabins.

Above the Saloon Deck was C Deck, the Shelter Deck. Crew's mess facilities and galleys in the bow gave way to a loading area well equipped with two electric cranes to service the cargo areas accessed via No. 2 hatch and the bunker hatch. Aft of this cargo handling area was first-class accommodation. In fact, all of the passenger cabins from this deck upward were devoted to first class. The majority of these cabins were suites with two bedrooms and their own private bathrooms, although the design allowed for an arrangement of interconnecting doors, offering a great deal of flexibility in the

way that the suites could be sold; White Star could, for example, offer a single-bedroom suite with its own bathroom and then offer the second bedroom as a private first-class cabin without bathroom.

Ultimate luxury

The most desirable of the suites were the staterooms, which could be booked with a room to be used as a drawing room, sitting room or even a private dining room. The sitting rooms were decorated in a most elaborate manner, mimicking the grandeur of a number of different styles and periods—Louis XV, Renaissance, Georgian, Queen Anne, Empire, Adam, Modern Dutch and Old Dutch. They were appointed with the finest-quality furnishings that suited the period and the walls were paneled with polished oak, mahogany or sycamore. To fit with the intended style—Adam, for example—the wall panels were painted accordingly, as were the decorative plaster moldings on the ceilings. Nowhere in any of these rooms would there be found any bare pipe or steelwork to betray the fact that this was actually a cabin aboard ship. The rooms even had mantelpieces above appropriately styled fireplaces to complete the effect. The beds were of brass, mahogany or oak, larger than in standard cabins, and had reading lights on the wall

Above left: The Promenade Deck, where first-class passengers could stroll, take the air and enjoy the sea views while remaining under the protection of the Boat Deck above.

Above right: The first-class Grand Staircase allowed passengers to make an elegant entrance to the reception room on D Deck leading to the first-class dining room, where groups would gather prior to going in to dinner. The Grand Staircase was capped at Boat Deck level with an ornate glass dome.

above the bedhead to complement the other electric wall and ceiling lights. Some were also equipped with electric ceiling fans and electric heaters.

Around the area of the grand staircase were the inquiry office and the purser's office, while moving aft from the grand staircase, there were suites to port and starboard with smaller standard first-class cabins on the inboard sides of the port and starboard corridors. It was envisaged that many of these cabins would be occupied by the servants of the first-class passengers traveling in the more expensive suites, and to that end provision was also made for a "Maids and Valets" saloon. The first-class barbershop was also in this section, and on the starboard side, above the hospital, was the first-class surgery.

Aft of the first-class section was the second-class promenade, an enclosed area of deck protected from the elements by a solid bulwark fitted with a long row of large

windows. This promenade was also one of the second-class entrance areas, there being another two decks below on E Deck and one up above on B Deck. Between the port and starboard promenades was another of the ship's most lavishly decorated spaces—the second-class library. The library had sycamore-wood paneling on the walls with a mahogany dado rail and mahogany furnishings. A large bookcase adorned the forward wall, while the bulkheads to the promenades outside had large windows draped with silk curtains. A Wilton carpet helped to maintain this as a retreat of peace and quiet.

The aft part of the enclosed port and starboard promenades included separate areas for "tourist" or third-class sheltered promenades, opening onto the open-deck area to the rear of the second-class library. This was the rear cargo-handling area, above which hung four electric cranes. The hatches here gave access all the way down to the refrigerated cargo hold on the Orlop Deck, but the deck surrounding the hatches was reserved as the first of the open-deck areas available for the use of passengers—the main third-class promenade. Through two sets of doors aft of the promenade was one of the third-class entrance areas, with another directly below on D Deck and one in the bow on E Deck. Naturally, the third-class entrances were nowhere near as grand as those enjoyed by

This page: Francis Browne took this photograph of passengers being seated in the first-class dining room.

Opposite: Devoid of passengers, place settings and table cloths, the extent of the first-class dining room is more apparent in this official Harland & Wolff photograph, as is the ornate plasterwork on the ceiling.

first-class passengers. The steel girders were flanked by their rows of rivets painted stark white, and the ceiling was formed not of lovingly crafted plaster moldings but from the white-painted steel plates of the deck above. Nevertheless, this was no ordinary immigrant ship; this was the *Titanic*, and provision had been made for the "steerage" passengers over and above that which they might expect on a lesser ship.

In the port-side entrance area, a small bar was planned, along with a large room taking up half the width of this stern section and designated as the third-class smoking room. This room had oak-paneled walls, teak tables and chairs, and a linoleum-covered floor, giving the impression of a large saloon bar. On the starboard side, opposite the smoking room, was another facility for third-class passengers—the common, or "general," room. This was a bright, popular room with white-painted, pine-paneled walls and teak benches, tables and chairs. It was intended as a meeting room for socializing and

relaxation, a piano stood against the back wall. The ship's musicians did not play here, but many other musicians undoubtedly did during impromptu sing-songs. (Not a room that would have been appreciated by the postal workers on board the *Olympic*!)

The final stern compartment on C Deck was a machine space designed mainly to house the equipment for operating the steering gear and stern capstans.

The next level up from C Deck was the Bridge Deck, also called B Deck. The farthest forward part of the bow of B Deck was the forecastle, where the anchor chains lay in the channels through which they ran, descending at one end into the chain lockers and at the other out through the hull to the port and starboard anchors. Despite the fact that these side anchors each weighed 8 tons, the *Titanic* was also equipped with a much larger center anchor. The center anchor was stowed in a cradle on the forecastle and could be deployed when required

to prevent the ship from dragging its side anchors in a strong current or tide. The center anchor weighed a colossal 50.5 tons. At the aft end of the forecastle was the forward mast designed, along with its twin 600 ft. (183 m) back in the stern section, to keep the radio aerial 30 ft. (9 m) above the funnels to avoid interference from exhaust gases.

Aft of the mast was the cargo handling well and then that part of Bridge Deck that was an integral part of the *Titanic*'s superstructure. Here the plans included a forward promenade for first-class passengers followed by a series of first-class suites up to the area of the grand staircase, where there was another first-class entrance. Aft of this entrance were the two most desirable suites on the whole ship. One was on the starboard side and one on the port side. Each was intended to have two bedrooms, a private bathroom and two "wardrobe" rooms (all of which could be found in many other first-class suites) plus a large sitting room and their truly unique feature— private promenade decks. Around 15 ft. (4 m) wide and 50 ft. (15 m) long, these fully enclosed promenades would come with cane deck chairs and loungers in which to relax while enjoying the view. Large windows looked out over the sea, and the ceilings were fitted with fake oak beams to match the oak-framed panels on the outside walls of the suites. These were

the *Titanic*'s most expensive suites, costing £870, and came with an inside first-class cabin for the use of a servant.

Traveling to New York in one of these suites was Mrs. Charlotte Cardeza and her son Thomas, who boarded at Cherbourg. Mrs. Cardeza's baggage included 14 trunks, four suitcases, three crates and a medicine chest. Her baggage included 70 dresses, 38 feather boas and 10 fur coats. Traveling with the Cardezas was their maid, Anna. The other promenade suite was occupied by J. Bruce Ismay, his valet and secretary, but it was originally booked for J. P. Morgan. Morgan canceled his trip at the eleventh hour, claiming ill health, allowing Ismay to take over the suite that had been designed to Morgan's specifications to be reserved for his personal use whenever he wished to travel.

A pavement café

The first-class suites that were designed to take up the mid-ships section of B Deck were slightly less spacious than the "promenade suites," but still lavishly appointed in one or other of the many period styles adopted aboard the *Titanic*. These ran back on the starboard side as far as what was intended to be the restaurant promenade outside the à la carte dining room. On the *Titanic*, this actually became the Café Parisien. A

Above left: The Café Parisien outside the à la carte restaurant on B Deck was designed to have the atmosphere of a pavement café in Paris and became extremely popular with younger passengers.

Above right: The *Titanic*'s gymnasium on the Boat Deck included apparatus that is still recognizable today, including rowing and cycling machines.

popular spot with the younger first-class passengers, this area was designed to have the ambience of a pavement café with wooden trelliswork on the walls—up which ivy or vines were intended to grow—and matching patterns in the woodwork on the ceiling. There were, of course, electric ceiling lights, but natural light flooded in through the large windows, giving the café what was described as "the appearance of a charming sunlit verandah." The cane furniture added to the outdoors look, although passengers choosing to dine here enjoyed the same standard of food and service as those in the à la carte restaurant.

The remainder of this section of B Deck, stretching all the way across to the port side, was devoted to the reception area, galley and pantry of the à la carte dining room, the dining room itself occupying the lion's share of this space. Decorated in the style of Louis XVI, the room was paneled in a light, yet richly textured French walnut with gilded details. The columns

supporting the plaster ceiling, with its delicately molded flower patterns, were encased in carved wood—again with gilded decorative detail and a rose-colored Axminster carpet covered the floor. Great attention to detail was paid in the design of the brass ceiling lights, door handles, hinges and general fixtures to maintain the period style, with the finely carved furniture in the same light walnut as the walls. The restaurant could seat almost 140 diners, who enjoyed a menu prepared by the Italian restaurateur Luigi Gatti. Gatti ran two fashionable Ritz restaurants in London—Gatti's Adelphi and Gatti's Strand. He was offered the opportunity to run the à la carte restaurant as a kind of franchise, and for the *Titanic*'s maiden voyage he brought with him his own chefs, maître d', manager and wait staff, who were mainly either French or Italian. Ten of his staff were his cousins, and this was to be their first ocean voyage.

Like the main dining room, the à la carte restaurant had its own reception room, decorated in a Georgian style with silk-faced sofas and armchairs in which to enjoy a predinner drink. Diners who chose to use the à la carte dining room instead of the first-class restaurant qualified for a rebate on their tickets (should those tickets have included meals) to compensate for the fact that they were paying extra for the experience of dining at Signor Gatti's establishment.

Gym wear in 1912 was a far cry from the figure-hugging Lycra of the 21st century. This couple is enjoying a leisurely cycle in front of the *Titanic*'s gymnasium clock.

Beyond Gatti's restaurant was an area earmarked as a second-class entrance and promenade with, between the port and starboard open areas, the second-class smoking room. The equal of any first-class public room on any other ship in the world, the *Titanic*'s second-class smoking room was paneled from floor to ceiling in carved oak with oak tables and chairs, the chairs upholstered in dark green leather. The linoleum tiles on the floor had been specially designed, and a fully stocked bar occupied on corner of the room.

The cargo-handling area took up the space aft of the smoking room, and at the stern of B Deck was the Poop Deck. This rounded stern deck and the decks immediately below it were designed to overhang the steering gear in the style of a schooner. The Poop Deck housed the stern capstans, two electric cranes for cargo handling and a stern bridge on a raised platform that was used to help guide the ship when docking. The open deck area was also designated as a third-class promenade.

The *Titanic*'s second-highest deck was A Deck, the Promenade Deck. Reserved for the use of first-class passengers only, the Promenade Deck was 500 ft. (152 m) long and up to 30 ft. (9 m) wide down the port and starboard sides. Although covered by the deck plates of the Boat Deck above, most of the promenade area was open, providing uninterrupted sea views. The Promenade Deck provided one of the most obvious visible differences between the *Titanic* and *Olympic*. Perhaps as a response to comments from passengers on the *Olympic* who had complained about being buffeted by the wind and soaked by sea spray, the forward part of the promenade deck was enclosed with a steel bulwark and glass windows that could be lowered in fine weather. The forward part of A Deck, surrounded by the enclosed section of promenade, was given over to smaller first-class cabins and a first-class entrance on either side of the grand staircase. Although it was not originally planned, a larger first-class cabin was also added on A Deck, and when the *Titanic* set sail for New York, this was occupied by Thomas Andrews.

Aft of the accommodation was the first-class reading room. Situated on the port side, this room's molded wood paneling was painted white, reflecting the light from the great bay window that looked out over the promenade. Furnished with well-upholstered armchairs for reading and more upright darkwood cushioned chairs for sitting at one of the many writing tables, this was considered to be very much a ladies' room. Adjacent to the reading room was the first-class lounge.

The ship's finest room

Of all the public rooms on the *Titanic*, this was the one to rival any of the world's top hotels. The polished wood paneling was adorned with exquisite carvings subtly lit by electric candelabra-style wall lights. Huge mirrors reflected light all around the room, and the ornate central ceiling light helped to display the finest plaster moldings anywhere on the ship. A magnificent fireplace with an over-mantel mirror stood at one end of the room, while against the opposite wall was an elaborate mahogany bookcase. Passengers could borrow books from here to take to the reading room next door or settle down in one of the many armchairs or sofas scattered around the room. There were tables for playing cards or writing, quiet alcoves for relaxed conversation and, naturally, instant steward service for morning coffee or an afternoon gin and tonic.

Beyond the pantry and bar intended to serve the lounge was the first-class smoking room. The dark mahogany panels lining the walls of this Georgian-style room were heavily carved and inlaid with mother-of-pearl. The panels surrounding the ventilation shaft that rose all the way up from the main engine room were framed ornate screens of stained glass showing sports scenes or representations of landmarks around the world that the *Titanic* might visit one day. Like the lounge next door, the smoking room had its own impressive fireplace and its own bar. The furniture, however, was far more robust and masculine, with winged leather armchairs and leather-trimmed seats surrounding the numerous card tables. If the reading room could be described as a ladies' room, then this room was undoubtedly one for the gentlemen.

Aft of the smoking room were the verandah and palm court. These areas were designed to further the impression that the *Titanic* was actually a floating country mansion. Trelliswork

similar to that in the Café Parisien was festooned with greenery, and walking through the doors from the smoking room into the verandah areas was intended to be like stepping out into a conservatory. Cane furniture and tables, along with linoleum tiles rather than the plush carpets in the lounge or smoking room, helped to foster this illusion.

Top of the ship

The final deck of the ship was the Boat Deck. In the forward section was the wheelhouse, the captain's cabin, officers' quarters and the Marconi radio telegraph room. It was here that the radio operator, Jack Phillips, and his junior, Harold Bride, listened for incoming messages and tapped out the Morse code signals being sent from the *Titanic* both to other ships and to shore stations within the equipment's 350-mile (563-kilometer) range. Phillips and Bride were afforded the rank of junior officers, but they were actually employees of Marconi rather than members of the ship's crew.

The top of the great glass dome, inside of which was suspended a glittering crystal chandelier, occupied the central deck space aft of the officers' quarters. Beyond that was another of the *Titanic*'s unique first-class facilities—the gymnasium. Situated on the starboard side of No. 2 funnel, the

gymnasium was paneled in plain white, the walls unadorned except for a map of the world showing White Star Line routes, an illustration of the *Titanic* with a deck guide and a large clock face. The gym boasted the most modern equipment. Some, such as the weight machines, rowing machines and cycling machines, would be immediately recognizable to anyone who uses a gym today. Other machines, such as the electric camel and electric horse might not be quite so familiar. Ladies could use the gym from 9:00 a.m. until 1:00 p.m., and gentleman from 2:00 p.m. until 6:00 p.m. Children were allowed in from 1:00 p.m. until 3:00 p.m. A visit to the gymnasium cost one shilling, and while exercising, passengers would be supervised by the *Titanic*'s fitness instructor, Mr. Thomas W. McCauley.

The remainder of the central section of the Boat Deck was taken up by the raised roof over the first-class lounge, on top of which was an isolated brass platform. Here one of the ship's compasses was kept free from any magnetic interference that might be caused by the iron and steel of the ship's structure. There was an officers' mess and other crew facilities, storage and the raised roof over the first-class smoking room. One of the storage areas at the base of No. 4 funnel was designed as a kennel for those traveling with their pet dogs. Along the port and starboard sides of the deck were promenades for the

Above left: Francis Browne took this shot of the first-class reading and writing room on the Promenade Deck.

Above right: Taking some exercise on the port side of the Boat Deck, the rear section of which was reserved for second-class passengers.

officers, first-class promenades amidships and second-class promenades to the stern.

The real purpose of the Boat Deck, of course, was for the boats. The boat deck was orignially intended to take 48 or even 64 lifeboats, but this number was reduced to give more space for the promenade areas and to avoid giving the impression that the ship was overloaded with lifeboats. Passengers were being assured that the *Titanic* was the most modern, safest ship afloat. Why then undermine their confidence by crowding the upper decks with lifeboats? The ultimate designs showed eight first-class lifeboats (and two small cutters) forward, and eight second-class lifeboats aft. The four Englehardt collapsible life rafts brought the total number of lifeboats on the *Titanic* to 20. The total lifeboat capacity was 1,176—only enough for around one-third of the 3,300 passengers and crew who could be carried on the *Titanic* when she was fully booked.

The *Titanic*'s design, even though she was the sister ship to the *Olympic,* was unique—as was the *Olympic's,* given the detailed differences between them. The *Titanic* was undoubtedly the most luxurious liner ever to put to sea, but at least some elements of her interior décor would have looked a little familiar to seasoned travelers. The interior design of many liners at that time was remarkably similar because adaptations of the same concept drawings would be used on different projects. Not all of the design work on the interiors was executed in-house by Harland & Wolff and the interior design contractors would certainly modify their drawings for the *Titanic* and then use them on other projects for which they were commissioned, just as the drawings for the *Titanic* and the *Olympic* may have been adaptations of earlier work. The materials used and the styles would echo earlier work.

Regardless of any such minor points, the White Star Line considered that Harland & Wolff had produced a package that met J. P. Morgan's demand for the "finest vessels afloat" when J. Bruce Ismay visited Belfast to review the drawings on July 29, 1908. After a formal presentation of the designs, he gave his approval and a contract was signed for the construction of the first two Olympic-class ships—Harland & Wolff keel numbers 400 (*Olympic*) and 401 (*Titanic*).

The *Titanic*'s hull begins to emerge from the scaffolding as she rests on Harland & Wolff's No. 3 slipway below the giant Arrol Gantry. Riveting her 30-ft. (9-m)-long hull plates to her framing skeleton took seven months and was completed in October 1910.

WHITE STAR
ROYAL MAIL STEAMER
"TITANIC"

CHAPTER FOUR

THE SHIPS
TAKE SHAPE

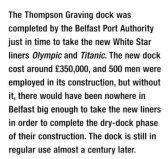

The Thompson Graving dock was completed by the Belfast Port Authority just in time to take the new White Star liners *Olympic* and *Titanic*. The new dock cost around £350,000, and 500 men were employed in its construction, but without it, there would have been nowhere in Belfast big enough to take the new liners in order to complete the dry-dock phase of their construction. The dock is still in regular use almost a century later.

The first problem shipbuilders face when they decide to construct the biggest ships the world has ever seen is where to build them. Obviously, the *Titanic* and *Olympic* were to be built by Harland & Wolff in Belfast. But were there facilities in Ulster big enough for the building of these massive liners? Could Harland & Wolff really cope with such an immense project? Moreover, once the ships entered service, would any port be capable of accommodating them?

In Belfast, preparations for the construction of bigger ships had actually been under way for many years. It was obvious to anyone involved in shipbuilding that shipowners were always going to demand bigger and better vessels. The Belfast Harbour Commission had long benefited from the advice of senior executives at Harland & Wolff. Sir Edward Harland had, after all, been its chairman, and Lord Pirrie had also served on the commission. Along with Gustav Wolff, they had both also been deeply committed to local politics, putting themselves in strategically advantageous positions to encourage the authorities in Belfast to provide the most modern facilities in order to promote the all-important local shipbuilding industry.

Some would have it that Harland & Wolff "bullied" Belfast's local authorities into doing whatever they wished. Certainly, had there been any lack of co-operation, Lord Pirrie would have been bullish enough to point out that Harland & Wolff could just

as easily build ships on the Clyde or the Tyne as they could on the Lagan. That would mean the loss of 15,000 Belfast jobs—plus those involved in ancillary or support industries. It is more charitable to assume, however, that the authorities in Belfast regarded the commercial well-being of Harland & Wolff and the livelihoods of many Belfast families to be so closely linked that whatever was good for Harland & Wolff was good for Belfast. The decision, therefore, of the Belfast Harbour Commissioners in 1902 to create a new dry dock bigger than any that had previously been built should come as no real surprise. The meeting between Lord Pirrie and J. Bruce Ismay in Downshire House, where they sketched out plans for their Olympic-class ships, was still four years away—but bigger ships were definitely in the cards, and Belfast needed to be able to compete with rival shipbuilding towns. In the end, the new dry dock would still be a fairly tight squeeze for the *Titanic* and *Olympic*.

Belfast's new dry dock

Belfast's new facility was to be called the Thompson Graving Dock, and contracts for its construction were issued in 1903, the three-and-a-half-year work schedule due to commence within a year. A civil engineering company from London—Walter, Scott & Middleton—was drafted in as the main contractor, although local Belfast firms were also involved in the £350,000

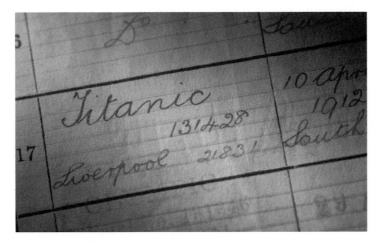

The *Titanic* was registered in Liverpool, although she was destined never to visit that port. The White Star Line maintained its headquarters in Liverpool but had moved its base of operations for the transatlantic trade to Southampton, from where the *Titanic* would set sail on her doomed maiden voyage.

project (in today's terms it would be worth about £50 to 100 million or U.S. $95 to 190 million at today's exchange rate), which at one time employed around 500 men. The dry dock was 128 ft. (39 m) wide at the top and 850 ft. (259 m) long, with a special outer door that could extend the overall length of the dock to over 887 ft. (270 m). Without that special provision, the *Titanic* and *Olympic* would not have fitted in. Millions of tons of concrete, brick and granite stonework were used to build the dock that had a floor and walls almost 20 ft. (6 m) thick. When it was flooded, 23 million gallons (105 million liters) of water poured in, but the dock's steam-powered pumps could empty it out again in less than three hours. The center of the dock's floor was laid with cast-iron keel plates topped with timber.

When a ship entered the dry dock, or graving dock (so-called because its shape resembled a grave), the gates would close behind it and the water would be pumped out in stages. The ship's keel would then settle on the keel plates, and as the pumps evacuated the rest of the water, props would be wedged between the ship's hull and the walls of the dock to hold it steady, repairs and maintenance to the hull or finishing work on a newly launched ship could then be carried out. Because the nearby Alexandra Dry Dock had collapsed mainly as a result of the work being done on the new Thompson Graving Dock, the project took almost twice as long to complete as expected, and the very first ship to enter the dock was the *Olympic* on April 1, 1911.

Hugely expensive dredging operations were also undertaken in the river opposite the Thompson Graving Dock to provide a depth of water that would allow bigger ships to be maneuvred in through the gates. Lord Pirrie knew that there would be a dry dock in Belfast for his new ships once they were launched, but what about their actual construction? How was Harland & Wolff to cope with the construction of these giants?

Harland & Wolff at Queen's Island consisted in 1908 of four areas: the Musgrave, Queen's, Abercorn and Victoria Shipyards. To provide for the building of the new ships, Lord Pirrie proposed that the three slipways in the Queen's Yard be demolished and replaced with two larger ones side by side. A third, smaller, auxiliary slipway was subsequently added during the building of the main two. The smaller slip became No. 1 slipway; the others Nos. 2 and 3. An enormous steel gantry crane system was planned to straddle the two main slipways.

The Arrol Gantry

Designed to specifications prepared by Harland & Wolff staff, the contract for the building of the gantry system eventually went to the Glasgow engineering company of Sir William Arrol. Arrol had built the Tay Rail Bridge, which was completed in 1887 (replacing the one that had collapsed so disastrously in 1879), and the Forth Rail Bridge, which opened in 1890. He had also been involved in the construction of London's Tower Bridge. The Arrol Gantry that was to span the Queen's Yard slipways Nos. 2 and 3 was a latticework of steel supported by three rows of 11 steel-girder columns. Almost 270 ft. (82 m) wide and 840 ft. (256 m) long, the gantry reached a height of 228 ft. (69 m). It was topped by a number of crane systems, including three moving frames over each slipway, and was served by four elevators as well as numerous walkways. This complex, 6,000-ton steel structure would dominate the Belfast skyline until it was eventually dismantled in the 1960s. The gantry was completed in time for the laying of the *Olympic*'s keel on No. 2 slipway on December 16, 1908.

Even though Harland & Wolff were committed to building the first two Olympic-class liners, other work at their complex continued. Of the 15,000 men the company employed, the construction of the *Olympic* and *Titanic* required no more than 4,000 each. The remaining workers were involved in other projects, not least the building of the White Star Line tenders,

On No. 2 slipway, work continues on the plating of the *Olympic*'s Tank Top with her stern framing takes shape at the far end of the gantry. Part of the *Titanic*'s bottom can be seen to the left on No. 3 slipway.

the *Nomadic* and *Traffic*. These two ships, each around 220 ft. (67 m) long, were destined to work in the French port of Cherbourg in Normandy.

The White Star Line maintained its headquarters in Liverpool, but had moved its base of operations for the transatlantic trade to Southampton. While they were both registered in Liverpool (the *Titanic*, in fact, was destined never to visit Liverpool), the *Olympic* and *Titanic* would sail from Southampton, calling at Cherbourg and Queenstown before heading out across the Atlantic to New York. The port facilities at Southampton could adequately accommodate the world's two largest ships, but their next port of call, Cherbourg, could not. Too big to approach the quayside, the liners would have to anchor offshore while the *Nomadic* and *Traffic* carried passengers, baggage and mail to and fro. The *Nomadic* was to carry the first-class and second-class passengers, while the *Traffic* carried third-class travelers, baggage and mail. There was a similar arrangement at Queenstown, with tenders the *America* and *Ireland* servicing the liners.

At their ultimate destination, New York, the White Star Line had requested that the port authorities enlarge the piers to allow the new ships to dock, but the request had been denied on the grounds that extending out into the Hudson River would constitute a danger to navigation. That danger suddenly evaporated when pressure was brought to bear on the authorities by J. P. Morgan. The man who could sway presidents, dominated Wall Street, ran U.S. Steel and owned a fair portion of the railroads was not about to let the city of New York's Port Authority stand in his way. White Star's superliners would have docking facilities in New York.

Titanic's keel is laid

No problem, it seemed, could stand in the way of the construction of the *Olympic*, and *Titanic*. Four months after work began on the *Olympic* the keel of Harland & Wolff ship 401, the *Titanic*, was laid below the giant gantry on No. 3 slip.

The keel is the spine of the ship, the main member from which the rest of the ship's structure will grow. The *Titanic*'s keel was made up of a central hollow steel box girder over 5 ft.

The *Olympic*'s keel was laid on December 16, 1908, four months ahead of the *Titanic*, although the *Titanic* would eventually be launched more than seven months after her sister ship.

(1.5 m) deep, mounted on a steel keel plate and reinforcing solid steel bar. More girders ran either side of this "spine" to create the bottom of the ship's hull with steel cross-members linking the girders. This entire framework was riveted together mechanically, using massive hydraulic pincers and half a million rivets—the rivets alone weighed 270 tons in total. Steel plates 1 in. (2.5 cm) thick were riveted to the bottom, sides and top of the frame. The "double bottom" thus formed was seen as a major safety feature—should the bottom plates be breached, water would penetrate only as far as the top plates.

The cross-member beams had circular channels cut through to create a honeycomb of compartments, or tanks, within the double bottom of the ship, although some were solid to create separations between the tanks. These tanks would be filled with water ballast to a greater or lesser degree when the *Titanic* set sail. Ballast is necessary to make a ship ride in the water at the right height. A lightly laden ship will sit higher in the water and be susceptible to the forces of the wind and waves, and so be more liable to bob around. To ensure a smoother passage, the ship takes on ballast that will allow it to sit lower in the water and thus be more stable. As the *Titanic* set out across the Atlantic, burning tons of coal per day and with food and fresh-water stores also being consumed, she would become lighter and ballast would have to be taken on to maintain her stability. Ballast could be pumped between tanks, if required, to balance with the weight of the water evenly, while bilge keel tanks 300 ft. (91 m) long to the port and starboard helped to stop the ship rolling in heavy seas. Its plating in place, this structure became the Tank Top.

From the bottom of the ship grew the side frames, the ship's ribs. Each was more than 60 ft. (18 m) high, and they were spaced at 3-ft. (91-cm) intervals along the length of the ship. At the bow and stern, the spacing was reduced even further. At each deck level, the deck beams were attached to the framing ribs and crossbeams were also added. These beams were 10 in. (25 cm) deep up to Lower Deck level, but slightly smaller above to prevent the ship from becoming top heavy. The crossbeams were supported by solid steel stanchions and pillars to make the entire framework of the ship an immensely strong grid of interconnected boxes. This was precision engineering—careful and methodical work that took more than a year until the *Titanic* was fully framed in early April 1910. The plating of the hull could then begin.

"Roof tile" hull plates

The plates used on the *Titanic* were 30 ft. (9 m) long by 6 ft. (1.8 m.) wide and 1 in. (2.5 cm.) thick. On the upper decks, the deck plating used was even thicker to increase the strength of the hull. The plates were attached to the framing along the ship's sides in strips called "strakes" and overlapped in a series of "joggles" when they were riveted together. This overlapping meant that the plates on the ship's hull resembled the slates on the roof of a house. Today the hull plates of a ship are butted together and welded for a smooth, streamlined finish, but in 1910 there was no alternative to riveting. The seams of the plates were double-riveted, while the butts were triple- or quadruple-riveted for extra strength, especially on the bottom plating. Once the riveters had finished their work, the caulkers turned their attention to key joints. On a wooden sailing ship, caulking had meant hammering tarred rope into gaps between the ship's planking or decking to make it watertight. On the *Titanic*, the caulker's job was to force a special putty into vulnerable joints using a high-pressure hydraulic pump.

By October 19, 1910, all of the ship's hull plates had been hammered into place, and the following day the *Olympic*, still several months ahead of her sister ship, was launched from No. 2 slipway. Although her plating was completed, the *Titanic* had some way to go before she was ready for launching. Certain sections of the hull would be pumped full of water to check that they were watertight. (If they could hold water in, they could keep water out.) Just before the ship's keel had been laid, orders were issued to the engine works for the manufacture of her boilers to commence. Subsequent instructions were issued as the hull took shape for other essential components, and a steady stream of components now began to arrive at No. 3 slipway, either from other parts of the Harland & Wolff complex or from outside manufacturers. The 15-ton stem anchor was delivered by local haulers, John Harkness & Co., on a steel-wheeled wagon pulled by a team of 20 horses. Each of the two side anchors weighed around 8 tons, and each link of their massive chains was 175 pounds (79 kilograms).

Specially cast steel brackets were delivered from the Darlington Forge Company to house the propeller shafts. The brackets for the port and starboard propellers held the shafts clear of either side of the hull and were plated over, forming streamlined "wings." The central propeller-shaft housing was situated farther astern than the two wing propellers and formed part of the sternpost casting that supported the ship's rudder. The sternpost was the "hinge" on which the rudder "door" pivoted to steer the ship. The central propeller turned immediately in front of the rudder, making the steering more effective because its thrust was deflected by the huge rudder. Also cast by the Darlington Forge, the rudder was manufactured in six segments, which, when fully assembled, created a blade 78 ft. 8 in. (23 m) high and 15 ft. 3 in. (4 m) at its widest.

The rudder was hung on the sternpost below the overhang of the Poop Deck, Shelter Deck and the sternmost part of the Saloon Deck. The steering gear required to turn the rudder was housed on the Shelter Deck and was, like all of the ship's equipment, built to a formidable scale. Even the rudder stock—the "axle" turned by the machinery—was almost 2 ft. (60 cm) in diameter. The steering gear was powered by two three-cylinder engines, either engine capable of doing the job alone with one as a standby. The machinery could be controlled either from the wheelhouse or from the docking-bridge above the Poop Deck.

The two sister ships grow side by side at Harland & Wolff's Queen's Yard. The height of the Arrol Gantry and the bulk of the ships it enclosed made them the dominant feature of the landscape for miles around.

The propeller-shaft housing formed part of the ship's hull, and like the rudder, some of the engine equipment and other essential fittings were installed while the ship was still on No. 3 slipway. When a ship is launched, it is far from complete—more an empty shell than a finished vessel—but the deck beams and plating form an integral element of the hull's strength and have to be finished to a certain degree before the hull hits the water. Clearly, maneuvring some of the bulkier equipment of the *Titanic* into place with so much of the structure already built would have been impossible, so some equipment was part-assembled and "sealed in" as construction progressed. It would have been equally impractical to install all of the ship's fixtures and fittings—especially the complete superstructure, funnels and masts—while she rested on the slipway. So, like every other ship, the *Titanic* would go to a fitting-out dock and then into a dry dock for finishing, subsequent to her launch.

Launch of the *Titanic*

The *Olympic* spent seven months after her launch being completed and fitted out. By that time, the *Titanic* was ready to be launched, and Lord Pirrie decided that unlike Harland & Wolff's usual ship launches, which were rather subdued events, that of the *Titanic* would be a very special occasion. On May 29, 1911, the *Olympic* was due to leave Belfast for two days of sea trials in order to be certified by the Board of Trade as seaworthy and fit to carry passengers. Before she left, the *Olympic* was opened to the public, and thousands stood in line to take a look around the luxury liner, paying up to 5 shillings for the privilege—a day's wages—all of which went to local hospital charities. When the *Olympic* returned fully certified, she was to stand as a spectator to the launch of her sister ship, the *Titanic*, which was attended by the new White Star tenders the *Nomadic* and *Traffic*.

The launch of the *Titanic* was advertised by the Harbour Commission in the local newspaper, and the public was invited to buy tickets for a specially reserved area at the Albert Quay that provided a perfect vantage point for the proceedings. The shilling each ticket holder paid was again donated to local hospitals and tickets could be purchased at numerous shops

The wooden props supporting the *Titanic*'s hull on No. 3 slipway had to be knocked away in sequence as part of the launch process before the ship could be released to slide into the water. This was dangerous work, and despite the use of hydraulic rams or triggers to hold the hull in place, making the props easier to remove, one worker died when some of the timbers collapsed on top of him.

around Belfast. It was not expected, however, that these would be the only spectators. Extra trams were laid on by the city corporation to cope with the crowds making their way down to the quaysides. Ferries and small steamers were running sightseeing trips out to the *Olympic*, anchored in Belfast Lough, and as the morning of May 31 wore on, crowds estimated at up to 100,000 gathered on the banks of the Lagan.

With the launch scheduled for 12:15 p.m., spectators with special Harland & Wolff invitations took their seats in the three purpose-built grandstands inside the shipyard. One of these stands was reserved for the scores of journalists who attended the launch, some having traveled all the way from America. The other two were for Harland & Wolff white-collar staff and guests of the company. A second grandstand, the owners' gallery, had been built for Lord Pirrie's most distinguished guests, who included Mr. and Mrs. McMordie, the Lord Mayor of Belfast and his Lady Mayoress; Thomas Andrews of Harland & Wolff; Mr. Sanderson, a senior executive with the White Star Line; J. Bruce Ismay and his family and the ship's ultimate owner—who had traveled from America just for this event—J. P. Morgan.

As befitting the grandest, most modern ship in the world, the *Titanic* was to be launched using the world's most modern launch system. Unlike the usual system, where all of the wooden props and supports that held the ship in place on the slipway were knocked away, albeit in a set order, until the ship moved

off down the slipway, the *Titanic* was held in place by hydraulic rams, or "triggers." These triggers took the strain off the props, making them easier and safer to remove before the triggers were released and the *Titanic* would slide gracefully into the water. To ensure that she actually did slide, the slipway was lubricated with 22 tons of a tallow-and-oil mixture.

At noon, with Lord Pirrie having left his guests to tour the slipway, check that the props had been removed and inspect the trigger mechanisms, a rocket was fired to warn any small craft in the vicinity that the ship's launch was imminent and that they should stay well clear. The *Titanic* flew a red flag from her stern as a further warning. Up on top of the Arrol Gantry, more cheerful flags were flying. The Union Jack and the Stars and Stripes flanked the White Star Line's red pennant with its white star, while a set of signal flags spelled out the message "Good Luck." At 12:10 p.m., a second rocket was fired as a five-minute warning and to signal that Harland & Wolff's gates were closing and that no one else would be allowed in. Finally, Lord Pirrie ordered the third and final rocket to be fired and the triggers were released. There was no bottle of champagne smashed over the bow to christen the *Titanic*, no naming speech, no fuss. She simply set off on her first voyage—which lasted all of 62 seconds. Two sets of drag chains weighing 80 tons each, and special anchors (not the ship's own) buried in the riverbed and attached via steel hawsers to eyeplates riveted to the *Titanic's* hull, slowed the ship from around 12

knots to a complete standstill before she had traveled more than half her own length.

As the cheers of the crowd subsided and the spectators began to make their way home, lunch was served for Lord Pirrie's most distinguished guests in the Harland & Wolff boardroom at Queen's Island. The press and other lesser guests were entertained with a lavish lunch at the Central Hotel in Royal Avenue, Belfast. At 2:30 p.m., the *Nomadic* delivered a small group of passengers that included Lord Pirrie, J. Bruce Ismay, J. P. Morgan and Thomas Andrews (as head of the Guarantee Group) to RMS *Olympic*, which left Belfast later that afternoon headed for Liverpool. Anchored in the Mersey, the *Olympic* played host to an inquisitive public before setting sail for Southampton and her first Atlantic crossing.

The *Titanic*, meanwhile, was detached from her chains and anchor hawsers to be ushered to her fitting-out quay by five tugs. Four of the tugs, the *Alexandra*, *Hornby*, *Herculaneum* and *Wallasey*, came from Liverpool's Alexandra Towing Company, while the fifth, the *Hercules*, was Harland & Wolff's own vessel. At the fitting-out quay was another new Harland & Wolff acquisition. The company had bought a floating crane secondhand from Germany to help install some of the heavy equipment on the *Olympic* and *Titanic*. It came with German workers to erect it and operate it while local men were trained— something that caused a great deal of friction in the shipyard.

This photograph shows work being carried out on the *Titanic*'s starboard propeller shaft and was taken by Robert J. Welch for Harland & Wolff. In order better to show the dimensions of the shaft and to balance the photograph more evenly, the photographer has doctored the photographic negative to remove one of the workmen who was standing second from the right. This created a "ghost" image.

When the *Olympic* was launched in October 1910, she was the first of White Star's planned three new superliners and the largest ship afloat. To show her off and ensure that she looked suitably impressive, she was painted white so that she would be clearly seen against the backdrop of the Arrol Gantry and the *Titanic*. The *Olympic* was later painted black like the *Titanic*.

At her own launch on May 31, 1911, the *Titanic* was painted black and is seen here being maneuvered toward the fitting-out dock.

The 200-ton crane could lift a weight of 150 tons up to 150 ft. (45 m) in the air and was essential for installing items such as the ship's boilers.

The power of steam

Slowly the mighty engines of the *Titanic* had taken shape. The ship's two conventional engines were of the triple-expansion type, which meant that the steam from the boilers was used three times. Steam entered the first, smallest cylinder, a mere 4 ft. 4 in. (1.3 m) in diameter, at high pressure and expanded, pushing down the piston inside the cylinder before escaping and being fed into the second, larger cylinder. There it would expand again, and the process was repeated. The pistons pushed down to turn a crankshaft, which then turned the pro-peller shaft with the equivalent of 15,000 horsepower—the same sort of power that might be produced by around 100 engines of the type used in a fast modern saloon car. This turned the three-blade propeller about 16 ft. (5 m) around 75 times a minute.

When the steam left the third cylinder, it was channeled into the ship's turbine engine, causing the turbine blades to spin and turn the central propeller shaft. The 16,000-horsepower output from the turbine could turn the central four-blade propeller, which was cast like the others in solid manganese bronze, at 135 revolutions per minute. All of this power would give the *Titanic* a service speed of just over 21 knots, with a top speed of up to 25 knots.

As the engineers and fitters worked on the ship's power plant, electrical engineers and electricians poured over her mass of electrical fittings. Electricity from the four 400-kilowatt generators was distributed via hundreds of miles of wiring to more electrical equipment than had ever been fitted to any ship. There were 150 electric motors powering equipment such as ventilation fans, 8 electric cranes, 10,000 lamps, 1,500 electric bells for passengers to summon stewards, illuminated signs in first- and second-class corridors, 520 electric heaters, irons, hot plates and other kitchen equipment. On the Shelter Deck just forward of the first-class entrance was an internal telephone exchange with 50 lines. The elevators used electricity, as did various service lifts in the pantries, and even the ship's whistles were electrically operated.

Also operable at the flick of a switch were the watertight doors of the *Titanic*. These were installed in the bulkheads running across the ship's lower decks that divided the hull into 16 watertight compartments. This was a safety feature, which, in the case of a serious accident when the hull was breached, would stop water from flooding into the whole ship. If water penetrated the hull, it would be confined to the compartment that had suffered the damage, and the *Titanic* was designed to stay afloat even if two compartments were completely flooded.

This was not a new idea, as Brunel had installed watertight compartments on his *Great Eastern* and *Great Britain* more than 60 years before. The trouble with watertight bulkheads, however, is that they form dead ends in corridors. Doors in the bulkheads, especially doors acceptable for use by passengers, form weak points where water will ultimately break through. But blank bulkhead walls across corridors on passenger decks are a major inconvenience. The White Star Line could not contemplate having its passengers being forced to climb stairways up to the deck above the bulkheads when trying to find their way around the ship. It was decided, therefore, that the watertight bulkheads would extend up from the Tank Top only as far as was practical. The lowest bulkhead reached only to the Middle Deck, the first deck wholly above the waterline.

The "unsinkable" myth

In the lowest part of the ship, the crew needed to be able to move from one compartment to another, particularly down in the boiler and engine rooms, and this is where the watertight doors were fitted. These were no ordinary hinged doors, but heavy portcullis-like structures based on a design developed by the German shipping line Norddeutscher-Lloyd. They were suspended above the doorways and would drop down into position, with hydraulic assistance if necessary, when the captain ordered the switch to be operated on the bridge. An electric alarm bell would then sound to warn that the doors were closing, a process that normally took 20 or 30 seconds. Crew members could also operate the doors using a hydraulic lever system, and an emergency closing system was in place

One of the watertight doors that were fitted in the *Titanic*. When open, the heavy steel door was held in position above the doorway, but at the flick of a switch on the bridge seven decks above, the door would drop down into place. It would also operate automatically should water in the compartment flood the floor to a certain level.

that would activate when water on the deck reached a certain level. A float would rise with the water until it tripped a switch that closed the doors. This system of watertight doors and compartments, along with the double bottom and the extremely robust construction of the ship led the press and the public to dub the *Titanic* "unsinkable," although this was not a claim ever openly made either by Harland & Wolff or the White Star Line.

Work on the *Titanic* had continued at a frantic pace throughout the summer of 1911. The upper superstructure, which included the bridge and the wheel house, officers' quarters, gymnasium and the raised roofs over the first-class public areas and the grand staircase, all took shape while belowdecks more equipment, such as the two refrigeration engine in the port engine room were installed. These units powered the refrigerated holds that were used for perishable cargo on the Orlop Deck, as well as the food stores on the Lower Deck and the various cold stores or larders in the galley and bar areas on higher decks. The system also allowed for the cooling of drinking water available from taps or fountains

throughout the ship and, ironically, for the making of ice.

The work gangs laboring on every part of the ship worked on specific tasks with specialists such as carpenters or cabinet-makers, who had manufactured banister rails or wood paneling coming aboard to install the pieces that they had made in Harland & Wolff's workshops. There was a "builder's specification book" running to more than 300 pages that was used as a guide for the furnishing and decoration of the ship. The guide was divided into sections covering areas such as "Castings, Decks, Lockers, Doors and Bulwarks" or "Plumber Work," "Ventilation and Heating" and "Cementing and Painting." Although the guide provided essential reference for the Harland & Wolff tradesmen, it was not followed slavishly. Harland & Wolff's foremen were masters of quality control and used their experience and authority to ensure that their workers finished every job—from a simple area of paintwork to the most elaborate carving or the installation of a stained-glass window—to the very highest of standards.

Great care was also taken with the more bulky installations, such as the ship's four colossal funnels. These left Harland & Wolff's workshops fully assembled and were transported to the fitting-out quay, where they lay in specially constructed cradles sitting on railroad bogeys. These ran on the network of tramlines that crisscrossed the shipyard. A steam engine, also running on the tramlines, pulled the heavily laden bogeys at crawling pace to the quayside. There, the giant floating crane plucked the funnels off their cradles, whereupon they were delicately swung into a vertical position before being lifted high above the *Titanic* and lowered onto the Boat Deck.

With autumn approaching and work progressing at a satisfactory pace, J. Bruce Ismay proposed that the *Titanic*'s maiden voyage should be set for the early spring of 1912. At that point, it seemed that there would be no problem in completing the *Titanic* in time, and the White Star Line duly announced on September 18, 1911, the sailing date of March 20, 1912, for its latest superliner. Two days later, the plan was scrapped. The *Olympic* had been involved in a fracas off the Isle of Wight and was coming home to Belfast with her tail between her legs.

Lord Pirrie, chairman of Harland & Wolff
(left), is pictured here with Captain Edward
John Smith on the deck of the *Olympic*.
Captain Smith commanded the *Olympic*
before taking charge of the *Titanic*.

CHAPTER FIVE

DELAYED DEPARTURE

On September 20, 1911, as the Royal Navy cruiser HMS *Hawke* was approaching Egypt Point on the Isle of Wight and heading up the Solent towards Portsmouth, her captain, Commander William Frederick Blunt, and his crew were observing the approach of the world's largest ocean liner, RMS *Olympic*. Roughly six times the size of the 7,500-ton *Hawke*, the *Olympic* made a fine sight as she began to pick up speed in the Solent. Having left her berth in Southampton at 11:25 a.m. with 1,313 passengers, the *Olympic* maneuvred into the Solent at the Calshot Spit buoy at 12:34 p.m. A few minutes later, she began to slow from around 19 knots to 11 knots in order to turn to port at the West Bramble Buoy and thus avoid the dangerous sandbank for which it was a marker.

It soon became clear that the *Olympic* and *Hawke* were attempting to navigate the same channel. It was equally clear that there was not enough room for them both. Commander Blunt ordered a course change, since the two ships were then running parallel to one another at a distance that was becoming alarmingly close. The *Olympic* then began to pick up speed. At this point, it seems that the wheel of the *Hawke* jammed just as an attempt was being made to steer the ship away from the *Olympic,* and she veered closer to the White Star ship instead. The *Hawke* was then caught in the wash from the *Olympic*'s bows and dragged towards the giant liner.

As it cuts through the water, every ship creates a kind of vortex to port and starboard, with the water that is pushed aside by its bow rushing back in again towards the stern. With the *Hawke* only a few hundred feet off the *Olympic*'s starboard side, less than a ship's length to the *Olympic*, a collision became inevitable. The *Hawke*'s bow slammed into the other ship's side, making a horrendous noise on impact and slicing two great gashes in her plating towards the stern—one above the waterline and one below. The steel of the *Hawke*'s entire bow section crumpled like tinfoil, and for a moment it looked like she might capsize. Miraculously, she remained upright. Both captains had ordered their watertight doors to be closed, both ships were severely battered, but both stayed afloat.

Who was to blame for the accident? With the *Hawke* having rammed the *Olympic*, at first it certainly looked as if

Commander Blunt would be held responsible for causing the collision. But a subsequent naval inquiry laid the blame squarely on the poor navigation of the *Olympic*. The inquiry, however, was still some way off as HMS *Hawke* limped into Portsmouth, where she would be repaired. The *Olympic* anchored off Osborne Bay, where her passengers disembarked by tender to the Isle of Wight. She then made her way back to Southampton, where a proper assessment was made of her damage. In the end, it took two weeks to effect the temporary repairs that would allow the *Olympic* to sail home to Belfast and the only dry dock big enough to accommodate her.

The New York incident

Alarmingly, the collision with the *Hawke* was not the only incident to mar the first few months of the *Olympic*'s service. The *Olympic* had left Southampton on her maiden voyage on June 14, 1911, arriving in New York via Cherbourg and Queenstown seven days later—although she managed the measured route used to time Atlantic crossings in 5 days, 16 hours and 42 minutes at an average speed of just over 21 knots. Her arrival in New York caused something of a sensation, not only for the crowds of onlookers but also for the owners of ships berthed at the docks. As the *Olympic* made her way to the newly extended Pier 59, the turbulence from her propellers caused a number of vessels to strain at their moorings. The tug the *O. L. Hallenbeck* was sucked towards the *Olympic*'s stern and the two ships made contact. This caused no more than a few scratches on the *Olympic*'s paintwork, but the tug owners claimed their damage was far more extensive and sued the White Star Line for $10,000. White Star countersued, but the whole affair ultimately petered out, the cases being dropped for lack of evidence.

The man in command of the *Olympic* during both the *Hawke* incident and the scrape with the *O. L. Hallenbeck* was Captain Edward John Smith. Born in Hanley, Stoke-on-Trent, in January 1850, Smith was the son of a potter and attended the Etruria British School up to the age of 13. He then went to Liverpool to pursue a seafaring career, and by 1869 he was an apprentice with the shipping line Gibson & Co. aboard their

The *Olympic* settled in the Thompson Graving Dock, showing her mighty three-blade port propeller, which was powered by a conventional engine, and the central four- blade propeller, which was turbine-driven. The three-blade starboard propeller is just visible beyond the central one.

command. He became White Star's preferred commander when a new vessel was being put through its sea trials or for a vessel's maiden voyage. His charming good nature made him a favorite with well-heeled passengers crossing the Atlantic. Some would even request when booking their passage to sail on a ship commanded by Captain Smith. Nor was he any less popular with his officers and crew, who were also keen to sail with the man whose rapport with his high-society passengers led to his becoming known as the "millionaires' captain." His crews referred to him affectionately as "E.J.," although, out of respect, not to his face. With a salary of £1,250 a year, Smith was the White Star Line's highest-paid officer and, as such, one of the highest-earning sea captains in the world.

Captain Smith sails on

The incidents with the *O. L. Hallenbeck* and *Hawke* did not reflect badly on Smith's career. Each incident had, after all, occurred when the ship was either entering or leaving port, at which point it was under the control of a local pilot. Smith's record was, in any case, as good as—if not better than—any sea captain at that time, which is why he was earmarked as the man to take charge of the *Titanic* on her maiden voyage. In October 1911, however, Captain Smith was in command of the world's largest damaged ship, heading for the Thompson Graving Dock in Belfast.

With the *Olympic* on her way north, work had to stop on the *Titanic* so that the dry dock could be flooded and she could be towed out and berthed. Because of the *Titanic's* draft, she could not be removed from dry dock until high tide, to ensure that there was enough water under her keel when she was clear of the dock. The last thing anyone wanted was for her to run aground. Similarly, the *Olympic* had to wait for high tide before she could be maneuvered into the dock. The extent of the damage and the need to get the *Olympic* back into service as quickly as possible meant that men had to be transferred from the *Titanic* to help with the repairs. Work on the *Titanic* did not grind to a halt completely, however. And even though the *Olympic* was laid up for repairs for six weeks, the scheduled date of the *Titanic's* maiden voyage was delayed by

American-built clipper *Senator Webber*. In 1880 he joined the White Star Line as fourth officer on the *Celtic,* and by 1887 he had his own command as captain of the *Republic*. That year he married Sarah Eleanor Pennington at St. Oswald's Church, Winwick, although the couple would spend little time together because Captain Smith was quickly becoming one of the White Star Line's most valued masters, in great demand for voyages not only across the Atlantic but also on the Australian run. He went on to command 17 White Star vessels, including the *Coptic, Majestic, Baltic* and *Adriatic.* With White Star sailing from Southampton to New York rather than from Liverpool, Smith left Merseyside to live closer to the port from which he would most often depart. He moved into an impressively large, brick-built house called Woodhead in Winn Road, Southampton, with his wife and their daughter, Helen.

Captain Smith's status within the White Star Line organization grew as the years went by. He served with distinction during the Boer War, commanding troop ships bound for South Africa, and earned the right, as a captain of the Royal Naval Reserve, to fly a blue ensign—rather than the merchant navy's red one—on any merchant vessel under his only three. The White Star Line announced that she would sail from Southampton on April 10, 1912.

Work on the completion of the *Titanic* continued throughout the autumn of 1911 and winter of 1912. More equipment and machinery were installed and tested—including, in the lowest part of the ship, the pumps in the boiler rooms. Pumps were used to supply the boilers with water and to circulate the water within the boilers as well as for filling, emptying or balancing the tanks to maintain an even distribution of ballast. Housed in separate, specially constructed chambers within the boiler rooms to protect them from ash or dust that might cause them to jam, the pumps were also used to discharge the ash and dust.

Burning over 600 tons of coal a day produced several tons of ash that had to be disposed of through ash ejectors. There were two ash ejectors in each of the five main boiler rooms. Ash was shoveled into the ejector compartment, the inner door was sealed and seawater was pumped in under pressure. An outer door, to the outside of the hull, was then opened and the ash was expelled into the sea (the boiler rooms, of course, being below the waterline). This was fine when the ship was way out in the Atlantic but not so desirable in port. There the ash was shoveled into bags and winched out of the boiler rooms on special ash hoists for disposal.

While machinery was being installed at the bottom of the ship, engineering works of a different kind were being incorporated into the *Titanic*'s superstructure. From the Bridge Deck upward, the ship was sliced into three sections by two expansion joints that ran the full width of the decks from port to starboard. These joints were to allow the ship to flex when riding rough seas. When the *Titanic* crested a high wave, momentarily, the center section of the ship might be supported by the wave while the bow and stern stood clear of the water. Gravity would then naturally cause the bow and stern to sag. Alternatively, the bow and stern might be supported by waves, causing the center section to sag into a trough. The steel used in modern ship construction is designed to be flexible enough to compensate for this phenomenon, but the *Titanic* needed the expansion joints—literally, vertical cuts through the top

The *Titanic* nears completion in the Thompson Graving Dock, with her funnels and masts in place and the German floating crane in attendance.

decks—to help her cope with the strain. The joints were patched with hinges of leather, steel and iron, allowing them to move, with the deviation over the *Titanic*'s entire 882 ft. 9 in. (269 m) of length amounting to only a few inches—certainly not enough for passengers to notice the ship "bending."

Logistics and supplies

A constant stream of material was now arriving daily at the dockside to be hoisted aboard the *Titanic*. Harkness, the Belfast haulers, delivered heavier items at a rate of just over a shilling a ton. Other local companies were also involved in the completion of the ship. Lumber merchants Irvin & Sellars supplied timber, as did James Corry; J. Ridell & Co supplied buckets while Robert Kirk delivered firebricks. Still more firms were employed in upholstering furniture or providing soft furnishings or linen. The *Titanic* would set sail with 45,000 table napkins aboard, 25,000 fine towels, 7,500 bath towels, 15,000 single sheets, 3,000 double sheets and 6,000 tablecloths. This represents just a tiny fraction of the *Titanic*'s housekeeping inventory but shows something of the logistical operation under way during construction to ensure the ship was fully stocked as she neared completion and was ready to depart on time—45,000 table napkins cannot, after all, be conjured up overnight.

Additional items scheduled to arrive for fitting included door handles, escutcheons, finger plates and other door furniture from London specialists N. Burt & Co. Locks, lamps and electrical fittings came from William McGeoch of Glasgow and beds and mattresses from the Birmingham firm of Hoskins & Sewell, although the Marshall Sanitary Mattress Co. of London also supplied their "Vi-Spring" line. All the while, an army of carpenters, decorators and plumbers toiled inside the ship. The tiles in the Turkish bath leisure suite were laid, as were the tiles for the swimming bath. Carpet fitters stretched and laid Axminsters and Wiltons over a thick underlay to soften the steel of the decks underfoot. Many of the tradesmen had never seen such luxury before. The crystal chandeliers being hung by the electricians cost more than the men earned in a year.

Olympic returns once again

Yet still there were delays. A boilermakers' strike during the *Titanic*'s fitting out had been accommodated more or less within the schedule, but it was the demands of her older sister that were really to throw a spanner into the works. On February 24, 1912, the *Olympic* was two days out of New York, heading eastbound across the Atlantic, when she hit something below the surface of the water and lost one of the blades on her port propeller. It has been speculated that the *Olympic* passed over a wrecked ship, but the navigation of the liner was called into question because most large wrecks that might pose a danger to shipping are marked on charts for their avoidance. In fact, there was no chance that the *Olympic* hit an actual shipwreck, because she was 750 miles (1,207 kilometers) off the Newfoundland coast, and the ocean there is several thousand feet deep. The *Olympic* could have passed over any shipwreck resting on the bottom without even coming close to scraping it. In any case, had she gone over such a wreck, damage would have been caused all the way along her hull, not just to one propeller in the stern. It is more likely that she hit what was known as a derelict wreck.

A derelict was the wreck of a wooden ship—or part of the wreck—that was not resting on the bottom but buoyant enough to be able to drift just below the surface. Such wrecks have been compared to semisubmerged logs, hanging in the water

like the corpses of long-dead ships. The turbulence created by the *Olympic* passing above one of these derelicts might have been enough to disturb it, perhaps causing it to rise up and strike the port propeller before the ship could escape. Obviously, no one could have foreseen any of this happening.

Whatever the *Olympic* hit was big and solid enough to shear off a propeller blade. The blade would have been expected to break off in the event of such a severe strike to prevent buckling and serious damage to the hull. Losing a propeller blade would, however, have been immediately noticeable. Seriously unbalanced, the propeller shaft had to be disengaged immediately; otherwise its violent vibrations would have started to shake its mounting to pieces, again running the danger of damaging the hull. The shaft and the port engine could also have been destroyed.

The *Olympic*, again with Captain Smith in command, continued her journey to Cherbourg and Southampton at a reduced speed. Arriving in Southampton on February 28, *Olympic*'s passengers disembarked, her cargo and mail were unloaded and she sailed for Belfast the next day with a reduced crew: Nonessential crew members such as restaurant staff, stewards, galley crew and certain of the seamen were paid off in Southampton, to be rehired when repairs were completed if they had not already joined another ship.

The *Olympic* arrived in Belfast on March 1 to find the *Titanic* still occupying the dry dock. With the next high tide, they then began jockeying for position, the *Titanic* being removed from the dock around 10:00 a.m. on Saturday, March 2, and anchored well clear of the *Olympic* as she was maneuvered into the dock. The *Titanic* then took the *Olympic*'s place at the fitting-out quay as the Thompson Graving Dock was pumped out so that the damage to the *Olympic* could be examined. It took no more than 24 hours to replace the missing propeller blade. But while the laborious process of removing the *Olympic* from the dry dock was under way, and with the *Olympic* being turned so that she was facing the right way to head out to sea and back to Southampton, the ship's hull grounded. Unbelievably, she had to be returned to the dry dock for inspection. The whole performance of the maneuvers and

The *Olympic* and *Titanic* were last seen together in Belfast in March 1912 when the *Titanic* had to be hauled out of dry dock and work on her was delayed while the *Olympic* was installed in the dry dock. The *Olympic* needed to have her port propeller replaced, having lost it after hitting an unknown object in the Atlantic 750 miles out of New York.

This was the view looking forward from the rear of the starboard-side second-class promenade area on the Boat Deck.

the draining of the dock had to be repeated. In the meantime, the *Titanic* had to wait alongside at the fitting-out quay until her sister ship was given the all-clear and sent on her way.

The *Olympic* finally left for Southampton on March 7 to meet a New York sailing date that had been delayed until March 13. Work could at last recommence on the *Titanic* to make sure that she was ready for her sea trials and a Board of Trade certification on April 1. Board of Trade inspectors had, in fact, been reviewing work on the *Titanic* at regular intervals throughout her construction, checking everything from the installation of her four compasses (two on the captain's bridge, one in the platform on the Boat Deck, and one in the stern docking bridge) to the slight camber on her decks designed to aid drainage. The *Titanic*'s Marconi radio was installed, connected to its twin aerial wires and tested. The radio could be run either off the main electricity supply from a backup generator or from a bank of batteries in the radio room. Both broadcast and reception appeared perfect, and the *Titanic* was given the call sign letter MGY.

The lack of lifeboats

Among the last items of equipment to be installed were the *Titanic*'s wooden lifeboats, all built by Harland & Wolff. Boats Nos. 1 and 2 were emergency cutters, 25 ft. (7.6 m) long and about 7 ft. (2 m) wide, with a capacity of 40. The other 14 boats were 30 ft. (9 m) long by approximately 9 ft. (2.7 m) wide and could take 65 passengers. These 16 boats hung from davits supplied by the Welin Davit and Engineering Co. The Welin davits were designed to swing the attached boat out over the side, lower it to the water and then swing back in again for another boat to be attached. The *Titanic* was intended to have two more boats per davit, but tragically, these were deleted from the final specification.

There were also four Englehardt collapsible boats, which had shallow wooden bottoms and canvas sides; these side "skirts" could be raised and fastened taut to form a boat that could hold up to 47 passengers. Two of these were stowed on either side of the officers' quarters and two on the officers' promenade.

In total, the *Titanic* had a lifeboat capacity of 1,178. This was well in excess of Board of Trade regulations, which stipulated that the *Titanic* need have provision for only around 960 lifeboat passengers. These regulations, however, were almost 20 years out of date, based as they were on the sort of overall passenger capacities of ships three or four times smaller than the *Titanic*. The *Titanic*'s lifeboat places represented a space for only about one in three of those who would be on board if she were carrying a full complement of passengers and crew. In the end, only 2,207 people would sail for New York—still twice the lifeboat capacity.

Despite the miracle of organization and planning that went into preparing the *Titanic* for her maiden voyage, there were still some items that would, quite literally, miss the boat. A large bookcase intended for the second-class library arrived too late It was sold and then resold, eventually ending up furnishing a civil service office.

Pride of Belfast

While there were some items like the bookcase that were not on board when the *Titanic* left Belfast, there were tradesmen working on the ship who would not have expected to be visiting Southampton. Harland & Wolff employees, adding final touches, finishing that last lick of paint, would still be hard at work as the *Titanic* headed south, and the White Star Line knew that they would be hard-pressed to have everything shipshape in time for the embarkation of passengers. The *Southampton Times and Hampshire Express* reported on this predicament on March 30, while the *Titanic* was still in Belfast:

The White Star berth will not be vacant very long after the *Olympic*'s departure on Wednesday, for the *Titanic* is due to arrive here on the same day. Whatever happens in regard to the coal trouble [a miners' strike was making coal scarce], the White Star Line are as certain as they can be that not only will the *Olympic* get away next Wednesday, but that the *Titanic* will be able to sail on her maiden voyage next week. The *Olympic* has picked up a large quantity of coal in New York, and the *Titanic* is assured of having her bunkers filled. The bookings for both sailings are heavy, and the departure of the two largest ships in the world from the docks within a few days of each other will be an event of considerable interest.

The officials have had so much worry lately that we gladly acceded to their request for our help in making it known that the *Titanic* will not be open for inspection. Already applications have been received from all quarters for permission to visit the ship, and the courteous "No" has been so often uttered that it was suggested that the services of a gramophone should be requisitioned at once! There is to be no pubic ceremony of any kind. The *Titanic* will enter the Solent without the blare of trumpets or the display of the silver oar. A lot of work will have to be done on board the ship during her week's sojourn at the Docks, and it will be impossible to allow people on board "except on business."

The public may not have been allowed on board but, perhaps in return for running the above announcement, a *Southampton Times* and *Hampshire Express* correspondent was given the opportunity inspect the *Titanic* and was suitably impressed. The following appreciation was printed on April 6, 1912.

In a port where the magnificence of the appointments of the *Olympic* are so well known, it seems scarcely necessary to say much about the *Titanic*. The privileged few who have had the pleasure of visiting the ship since her arrival at Southampton on Thursday morning have been at a loss to express their admiration. One person said that the *Olympic* was all that could be desired, and the *Titanic* was something even beyond that! And if his hearers smiled at his method of putting it, they were to agree that the White Star Line had taken every possible opportunity of effecting improvements, their experience with the *Olympic* having been brought to bear. The *Titanic* had a delightful trip from Belfast to Southampton, and among those on board were Mr. Morgan (Morgan,

Grenfell and Co.), and representatives of the London and Southampton offices of Café Parisien.

These gentlemen were quick to notice that several changes had been made in the *Titanic*, and particularly was it noticed the increased stateroom accommodation had been provided. The two private promenade decks were inspected with interest, and they have been instituted in connection with the parlor suite rooms. Then a delightful addition is the Café Parisien, which has been arranged in connection with the restaurant. The deck space outside the restaurant has been utilized for it and it represents an entirely new feature on steamers.

The Café Parisien has the appearance of a charming sunlit verandah tastefully arranged with trelliswork, and chairs in small groups surrounding convenient tables. It will also form a further addition to the restaurant, as lunches and dinners can be served with the same excellent service and all the advantages of the restaurant itself.

In the first-class dining room over 550 passengers can dine at the same time and a feature of the room is the arrangement of the recessed bays where family and other parties can dine together in semiprivacy. The second-class passengers have been very generously provided for. The dining saloon extends the full breadth of the vessel, and will seat 400. The staterooms are of very superior character and the promenades are unusually spacious, a unique feature being the enclosed promenade. The accommodation for third class is also very good, and the vessel will accommodate in all about 3,500 passengers and crew.

Although very few of them would have seen this review, everyone in Belfast was justifiably proud of the quality of the workmanship that had gone into the *Titanic*. Indeed, RMS *Titanic* was hailed in some contemporary reports as "The Pride of Belfast." The people of Ulster sorely needed such an inspiration, a symbol of hope as growing social and political unrest began to dominate their lives.

This photograph was taken from the
tender *America* as she pulled alongside the
Titanic, which had just anchored off
Queenstown. Captain Smith can be seen
quite clearly looking down from the
highest visible point on the *Titanic*.

CHAPTER SIX

PRIDE OF BELFAST

That the people of Belfast took pride in the *Titanic* and the other ships built at Harland & Wolff is beyond doubt, but not everyone felt quite so warmly about the company itself. A significant proportion had good reason to bear a grudge against the company, and this bad feeling has its roots in the sectarianism that has for so long been endemic in the everyday life of the people of Ulster. The Protestant/Catholic religious and political divide affected Harland & Wolff just as it affected every other employer in the province. Harland & Wolff was always seen as a "Protestant" employer, although the company would always deny that this had ever been official policy. In reality, however, throughout its history only a fraction of the workforce at Harland & Wolff was Catholic. Even in 1992, with most of the modern antidiscrimination laws in place, just 5 percent of the workers were Catholic.

There are historical reasons for the imbalance. The shipyard is in East Belfast, traditionally a Protestant area, and workers were recruited locally. Workers were also recruited on recommendation. If your father, uncle or cousin worked at the yard, he could vouch for you when a job vacancy arose, and Harland & Wolff, like many employers, would take the family connection as a strong reference. The strength of family ties meant that new recruits would work hard and behave well in order not to let down their relatives. Recruiting in this way meant that the skills required in the shipyard stayed within the Protestant community of East Belfast.

With the domination of Protestants in the workforce, there was very little sectarian disruption within the yard and the minority Catholic element found that most of their colleagues were happy to work alongside them. There was always a small, hard-core element, however, that found it difficult to accept the presence of Catholics, and at times when tension within the community was at its worst, they suffered severe prejudice—a trend that dragged on into recent times. In 1970, as trouble flared on the streets of Belfast and a spate of shootings erupted, a group of around 100 Harland & Wolff workers scoured some of the workshops, chasing known Catholics off the premises; in 1994 a Catholic worker, Maurice O'Kane, was shot dead at the yard.

During the building of the *Titanic*, when Lord Pirrie was in charge, there was a great deal of unrest among the Protestant workforce about Lord Pirrie's support for Home Rule. The Orange Order was especially concerned about his intentions. Politics and religion for the Protestant majority were largely dominated by the Orangemen, whose history dates back to the roots of sectarian unrest in Ireland.

Ireland's troubled past

Irish history is fraught with turbulence, right from the earliest times when the island was made up of a patchwork of small kingdoms whose rulers were constantly battling with each other over land, livestock and long-standing family feuds.

Wars between ruling factions in Ireland continued, with various kings vying for supremacy until King Dairmait Mac Murchada was driven out of Ireland in the twelfth century. He sought help in England, where he raised an army of Anglo-French noblemen with the blessing of the English king and the pope in Rome. Thus began the English involvement in Ireland, which became—with papal approval—a province under English administration, subject to English law and paying English taxes. There then ensued centuries of rebellions and uprisings until, in the middle of the fifteenth century, English influence in Ireland was reduced to an area only about 20 miles (32 kilometers) in extent surrounding Dublin. This area was known as the Pale and was fortified by the English, who built a fence around its circumference to keep the Irish out. It is from here that the expression "beyond the pale" derives.

The Pale had its own parliament in Dublin, extending its authority over the next few years until Henry VIII took the throne in England. Quelling yet another rebellion, he made peace with the Irish kings, now known as "lords," gaining control of most of Ireland. In 1541 Henry rejected the Roman Catholic Church when the pope would not grant him permission to marry Anne Boleyn, installing himself as head of the new Church of England. Irish churches were ordered to change allegiance to acknowledge Henry above the pope, but many refused, bringing Ireland's great religious divide into being. Settlers from England and Scotland were sent to colonize Ireland to give

Lord Charles Beresford, Frederick Smith and founder of the paramilitary Ulster Volunteer Force, Edward Carson, head a protest rally against Home Rule at City Hall, Belfast, for the signing of the Covenant on Ulster Day, 1912.

successive English rulers political and religious control over what was regarded, by the time of Queen Elizabeth I, as an English colony. Irish people were driven out of their homes, perpetuating the Irish cycle of repression and violent revolution.

In 1641, just as events in England were about to plunge the country into civil war, an uprising in Ulster led to the massacre of up to 15,000 Protestant settlers. Eight years later, the English king Charles was beheaded, and Oliver Cromwell assumed the title of Lord Protector of the Commonwealth of England. He had waited a long time to avenge the deaths of the Ulster Protestants and headed for Dublin with an army of 12,000 men. Bent on revenge and determined to achieve the suppression of the Irish, Cromwell's troops were given free rein to commit countless outrages: Thousands were slaughtered in a campaign that lasted a year. Cromwell harbored a bitter hatred of Catholicism and also expelled around 1,000 Catholic

priests from Ireland during this period, as well as instigating another of what would today be called "ethnic cleansing" programs—removing Irish from their homes to give their land and property to his trusted followers.

Battle of the Boyne

In 1689, when the English parliament invited the Dutch nobleman William of Orange to become king in place of King James II, whose Catholic faith it distrusted, James fled to France. He staged his comeback via Dublin in 1689, the decisive battle taking place on the banks of the Boyne River in County Meath in July 1690. In the Battle of the Boyne, Protestant settlers from the North fought Irish Catholics, and James's army was routed. His surrender came in Limerick over a year later, where punitive laws were imposed reducing Catholics in Ireland to second-class citizens, banning them from professional occupations, owning land or having an education.

Over the next 100 years, some civil rights were gradually restored to Catholics. But alarmed at the way their position of superiority was being eroded, Protestants formed the Orange

The *Titanic* was towed out to commence her sea trials at 6:00 a.m. on April 2, 1912. She had been due to undergo the trials the previous day, but high winds had caused a postponement.

Captain Smith with the *Titanic*'s officers: (back row, left to right), Chief Purser Hugh McElroy, Sixth Officer James Moody, Third Officer Herbert Pitman, Fifth Officer Harold Lowe, Fourth Officer Joseph Boxhall; (front row, left to right), Second Officer Charles Lightoller, Chief Officer Henry Wilde, Captain Smith, First Officer William Murdoch.

Order in County Armagh in 1795 in the memory of William of Orange and to demonstrate Protestant loyalty to the British monarchy. As Catholics began to demand equality and even Irish independence from Britain, the Orange Order grew strong on the feelings of insecurity among Irish Protestants. The Orangemen used their July Marches—supposedly in remembrance of the Battle of the Boyne—as an excuse to intimidate Catholics, and violence inevitably ensued.

The anti-British feeling among the Irish Catholics was exacerbated by the crop failures of the mid-nineteenth century, which led to widespread famine, a problem that the British government was not felt to have done enough to alleviate. An Irish Republican Brotherhood, known as the "Fenians," was formed to bring about an independent Irish state by force.

By the time the *Titanic* was under construction in Belfast, elements of the British government were trying to introduce Home Rule to Ireland, although the Irish Republican Brotherhood had formed a political party that rejected this policy outright, calling for a fully independent Irish nation. When Winston Churchill visited Belfast in 1912 as Lord Pirrie's guest

to speak at a meeting of the Ulster Liberal Association, he spoke in favor of Home Rule. Churchill's grandfather, the duke of Marlborough, had been made viceroy of Ireland in 1876, and young Winston had moved to Dublin, where his father worked as secretary to his grandfather. Winston's father, Lord Randolph Churchill, a conservative MP, had spoken out against previous attempts to bring in Home Rule, coining the phrase "Ulster will fight—and Ulster will be right" in the knowledge that the Protestant North regarded being ruled from Dublin as totally unacceptable.

"Home Rule Means Rome Rule" was one of the slogans used by Protestant marchers airing their fears that a Dublin parliament would be dominated by Catholics. Thus Lord Pirrie, who chaired the meeting at which Churchill spoke before accompanying him through the town—where he was jeered by angry mobs and reportedly pelted with rotten fish as he boarded the steamer to take him back to the mainland—found himself in charge of an organization that employed thousands of workers who despised his political views.

The religious and political tensions in Belfast and throughout Ireland reached a peak during World War I, when the Irish Republicans staged a rebellion on Easter Monday 1916 that would eventually lead to the partition of Ireland. The climate on the streets of Belfast while the *Titanic* was taking shape was,

This photograph was taken by Francis Browne aboard the *Adriatic* some time prior to his trip on the *Titanic*. The picture shows two Marconi wireless operators, the one on the left being Jack Phillips, who stayed at his post on the *Titanic*, sending the distress signal and the ship's position right to the end.

therefore, highly volatile. But the community that was seen to be tearing itself apart could justifiably point to the world's largest, most advanced ocean liner and reassure itself as well as the outside world that it was capable of producing more than just a turmoil of bitterness and hatred. The "Pride of Belfast" may have meant more to some of the city's residents than others, but the *Titanic* certainly represented a symbol of hope as a marvel of grace and beauty emerging from a country in such terrible conflict.

Titanic's sea trials

On April 1, 1912, the *Titanic* was due to undergo her sea trials, but high winds forced a postponement until the following day. Even though she left her berth as early as 6:00 a.m., a crowd of onlookers gathered to watch her depart. With Captain Smith in command and Board of Trade inspector Francis Carruthers on board, the *Titanic* headed out into Belfast Lough. Smith's senior officers were Chief Officer Henry Tingle Wilde (age 39), who had sailed with Captain Smith on the *Olympic*, First Officer William McMasters Murdoch (41), Second Officer Charles Herbert Lightoller (38), Third Officer Herbert John Pitman (34), Fourth Officer Joseph Groves Boxhall (28), Fifth Officer Harold Godfrey Lowe (28) and Sixth Officer James Paul Moody (34). The captain had another crew of around three dozen, along with almost 80 firemen and trimmers (coal workers)—sufficient manpower to crew the ship for the 12 hours of trials.

Once out in open water, the *Titanic* began a series of maneuvers, coming up to speed, then stopping, then executing turns at a variety of speeds, while Inspector Carruthers made notes on the performance of the ship and its equipment. A series of snakelike, port-starboard turns to test the *Titanic*'s handling were performed, and the engines were run with the port propeller at full astern while the starboard one was at full ahead before the Inspector was invited to join Captain Smith for lunch in the first-class dining room. An emergency stop was scheduled after lunch, and the *Titanic* took an acceptable 850 yds. (777 m) to come to a halt from 20 knots. She then headed out into the Irish Sea for a 40-mile (64-kilometer) cruise to monitor prolonged straight-line performance.

During this and the return trip, the *Titanic* touched 21 knots for short periods but was not expected to test her new engines to their full potential until they had been run in service for a while. With good weather, the ship could be expected to achieve her full speed of around 24 knots on her first Atlantic crossing.

The Marconi operators Jack Phillips (24) and his assistant Harold Bride (22) were also on board, running various tests on the radio equipment and sending and receiving Morse messages (they were not yet equipped with a radio with a speech function). Inspector Carruthers examined everything from the safety equipment and lifeboats to the water distillation facilities, the operation of the anchors and the certificates of the senior crew members and engineers before authorizing the *Titanic*'s passenger certificate and presenting a bill for his services.

Opposite: Francis Browne photographed these passengers boarding the *Titanic* from the tender *America* off Queenstown, Ireland, on the morning of April 11, 1912.

This page: Browne also captured this image of passengers watching the unfolding drama as the *Titanic* left Southampton when her wash caused the liner *New York* to break free from her moorings and be drawn into a near collision.

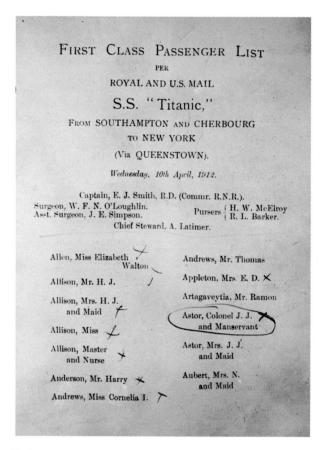

FIRST CLASS PASSENGER LIST
PER
ROYAL AND U.S. MAIL
S.S. "Titanic,"
FROM SOUTHAMPTON AND CHERBOURG
TO NEW YORK
(Via QUEENSTOWN).

Wednesday, 10th April, 1912.

Captain, E. J. Smith, R.D. (Commr. R.N.R.).
Surgeon, W. F. N. O'Loughlin.   Pursers { H. W. McElroy
Asst. Surgeon, J. E. Simpson.   { R. L. Barker.
Chief Steward, A. Latimer.

Allen, Miss Elizabeth   Andrews, Mr. Thomas
              Walton
Allison, Mr. H. J.   Appleton, Mrs. E. D.
Allison, Mrs. H. J.   Artagaveytia, Mr. Ramon
      and Maid
                               Astor, Colonel J. J.
Allison, Miss   and Manservant
Allison, Master   Astor, Mrs. J. J.
      and Nurse   and Maid
Anderson, Mr. Harry   Aubert, Mrs. N.
                                    and Maid
Andrews, Miss Cornelia I.

The first sheet of the *Titanic*'s alphabetical listing of first-class passengers.
The name of Colonel John Jacob Astor, one of America's richest men, has been
circled, perhaps to ensure he receives special attention.

The boiler-room fire

The *Titanic* was now ready to go into service and was officially
handed over by Harland & Wolff to the White Star Line. There
was no time for Thomas Andrews and his guarantee group to
spend time ashore, however, since a quick turnaround was
required when the *Titanic* returned to Belfast. She needed the
high tide at midnight the next day in order to dock at
Southampton, so she left Belfast for good at 8:00 p.m. on April
2, 1912. Her anticipated stop at her home port of Liverpool,
where she was to have been opened to the public, was
canceled to ensure that she made the tide at Southampton.

Only one incident marred the journey south: a fire was
discovered in one of the coal bunkers in No. 6 boiler room. This
was not an uncommon occurrence on ships of the time, and it
certainly was not allowed to delay the journey. Several trimmers
were assigned to remove the coal from the bunker. The
trimmers' regular job—shifting coal manually from one bunker or
hold to another to maintain a proper balance or trim throughout
a ship's journey as the coal was consumed—was one of the
dirtiest and most arduous jobs on the ship. Fighting a fire at the
same time was definitely no bonus. The fire stubbornly
continued to burn until the bunker was completely emptied of
coal, a process that took a full week. Technically, then, not only
was the *Titanic* on fire when she docked at Southampton but
also for the whole six days she was berthed there!

There was some concern that a national coal strike might
hamper the plans for the *Titanic*'s departure; in fact, other liners
had been forced to cancel voyages due to severe shortages.
Fortunately, the strike ended a few days before she was to sail,
and coal was also transferred from other White Star ships to
ensure that the *Titanic* would have enough. By the morning of
April 10, 1912, the *Titanic* was fully crewed, fueled and
provisioned—her larder was stocked with enough food to feed
an army and included 75,000 pounds (34,000 kilograms) of
fresh meat, 25,000 pounds (11,340 kilograms) of poultry and
game and 40 tons of potatoes—and she awaited the arrival of
her passengers before embarking on her maiden voyage. These
stores were just part of the provisions required to feed more
than 2,000 passengers and crew and included the raw
ingredients for the last first-class dinner served aboard the
Titanic. On April 14, the wealthiest passengers aboard sat
down to a feast that started with an hors d'oevre course of
canapés à l'amiral or oysters à la russe followed by a second
course of consommé Olga or cream of barley soup. There
was then poached salmon with mousseline sauce and an
entrée course of filet mignon Lili or sauté of chicken Lyonnaise
or for non-meat eaters, vegetable marrow farcie. Next came
a choice of lamb with mint sauce or Calvados-glazed roast
duckling with apple sauce or roast sirloin of beef forestière,
all served with a selection of vegetables, boiled rice or
potatoes. There was also a punch Romaine followed by roasted

squab on wilted cress and then cold asparagus salad with Champagne-saffron vinaigrette. If they still had room, the *Titanic*'s elite could then have pâté de foie gras followed by a desert of Waldorf pudding, peaches in Chartreuse jelly, chocolate-painted eclairs with French vanilla cream or French vanilla ice cream. To round off the banquet, there was a selection of fresh fruit and cheese. Each course was, naturally, accompanied with the appropriate fine wines, which, like the cuisine, were of the standard one would expect at the finest restaurants in London or Paris.

The maiden voyage

Since there was reportedly one passenger on board who had booked from Belfast to New York, as well as a load of mailbags, the *Titanic*'s maiden voyage was technically Belfast-Southampton, but this small detail mattered very little to those passengers who began arriving at 9:30 a.m. on April 10 for what everyone regarded as the maiden voyage of the world's greatest superliner. The boat-train from London Waterloo disgorged 497 third-class and 245 second-class passengers, all eager for their first glimpse of the largest ship on earth. The 202 first-class passengers arrived on a later first-class train, but all of the passengers and their baggage were on board in time for the *Titanic* to sound her whistles and depart for Cherbourg at noon sharp under the temporary guidance of harbor pilot George Bowyer. The ensuing incident with the *New York*—when the *Titanic* surged past the smaller, berthed liner causing her to break her moorings and come close to colliding—was severely embarrassing for George Bowyer. He had also been the pilot on the *Olympic* when she collided with HMS *Hawke*.

Six and a half hours later, the *Titanic* dropped anchor off Cherbourg. The tenders *Nomadic* and *Traffic* delivered some notable first-class passengers, who included the famous fashion designer Lucy, Lady Duff Gordon (whose fashion house "Lucile" was in London's Hanover Square, just off Regent Street) and her husband, Sir Cosmo Duff Gordon. Also coming aboard was the American mining tycoon Benjamin Guggenheim, whose personal fortune was said to be worth over $50 million. In the first-class dining room that evening they would join society figures who had embarked at Southampton. These included Colonel John Jacob Astor IV, reputed to be worth over $85 million, whose real estate empire was said to include a large portion of Manhattan. The 46-year-old entrepreneur had recently divorced and remarried and had left the United States on an extended honeymoon with his second wife, Madeleine, who was just 18. They had been the talk of New York. Now they were certainly the talk of the *Titanic*.

The banker George Widener, whose fortune was estimated at around $30 million, was returning to the United States with his wife and son, while Isador Straus, who owned the New York department store Macy's, was returning from a holiday in Europe with his wife, Ida. Then there was the steel magnate Arthur Ryerson and his wife, the railroad and hotel tycoon Charles M. Hays with his wife, Margaret, and daughter, Clara, and the special military adviser to the U.S. president, Major Archibald Butt. The *Titanic*'s first-class passenger list would have taken up quite a chunk of a U.S. *Who's Who*—one of the major reasons why her sinking caused such a furor in newspaper reports around the world. Nothing makes a newspaper story work better than a liberal sprinkling of references to untold wealth.

Over 140 first-class passengers and 130 second- and third-class passengers joined the *Titanic* at Cherbourg, with 22 passengers (all either first or second class) disembarking, having enjoyed an eventful and expensive Channel crossing. The transfer of passengers, baggage and mail took a little over 90 minutes before the *Titanic* was on her way again, headed for Queenstown. The tenders *America* and *Ireland* were waiting for the *Titanic* when she arrived at 11:30 a.m. on Saturday, April 11, as were a number of small boats. Enterprising Irish traders had taken to the high seas to try to tempt the *Titanic*'s wealthier passengers to buy their wares during the two hours the *Titanic* would be anchored off Queenstown. The tenders brought over 100 third-class passengers, a handful of second-class travelers and 1,385 sacks of mail, which were exchanged for seven first-class passengers who had bought tickets to take them from England to Ireland. Once their business was done, Captain Smith prepared to take the *Titanic* out into the Atlantic.

The *Titanic* bade her last farewell to her native Ireland two hours after she arrived from Cherbourg. As the passengers watched the Irish shoreline fading into the distance, they could not have known that two-thirds of them would never live to see dry land again.

With the Irish coast near Queenstown lying off her bow, the *Titanic* raises her anchors for the last time as she prepares to head out into the Atlantic.

CHAPTER SEVEN

ATLANTIC CROSSING

With the hawkers' small boats pulled well clear, the *Titanic* engaged her mighty engines and headed out into the Atlantic at 1:30 p.m. to the sound of a bagpipe lament played by third-class passenger Eugene Daly, who had boarded at Queenstown. Daly may have lamented the fact that he would never see Ireland again, but he was one of the lucky ones who would survive to see America.

Captain Smith took the *Titanic* out into the southern sea lane, long designated as the safest route to take when crossing the Atlantic in all but the warmer summer months. This route should have allowed him to make the crossing avoiding any danger of the freezing temperatures and ice floes found farther north. Unfortunately, the late winter and spring of 1912 had been sufficiently mild to cause enormous ice floes to break away from the ice shelf in the far north and drift south.

Each spring many thousands of major icebergs detach themselves from the Arctic ice shelf as the weather warms and the ice retreats northward. These slowly melt, breaking up into fields of smaller ice as they move south. Only a few hundred large icebergs ever make it as far south as the *Titanic*'s route each year, but an unusually high number had been reported by other shipping a week before the *Titanic*'s Atlantic voyage. Nevertheless, the *Titanic* was enjoying mild weather and calm seas, making almost 520 miles (837 kilometers) on her second day out from Queenstown and another 546 miles (879 kilometers) by midday on Sunday, April 14.

By the Sunday, the passengers had settled into the routine of their voyage, strolling on the decks or, for first-class passengers, enjoying the leisure and sports facilities. Sunday morning was slightly different in that there was a church service held in the first-class dining room. After that, there was time to relax before lunch and then perhaps enjoy some bracing sea air before taking tea in the lounge and listening to a trio from the ship's band play a mix of classical and popular music. Second and third-class passengers did not enjoy the luxury of a musical interlude during the afternoon. The highlight of the day, of course, was socializing before, during and after dinner. First-class passengers were expected to dress formally for dinner, the gentlemen in black tie and evening suits, the ladies in their most elegant gowns. It was important to be seen attending dinner, so first-class passengers with cabins on the lower decks would take the elevator up to the top of the grand staircase in order to make an entrance by walking down the staircase to the reception area. The idea, then, was to rendezvous with new friends met during the day and enjoy cocktails before going in to dine. Afterward, the band would play for dancing, although not on Sunday, as it was White Star Line policy not to have dancing aboard ship on the Sabbath. The social scene was slightly more relaxed in second class and positively informal in third class, where the passengers were encouraged to retire early.

Reports of icebergs

With the passengers enjoying a calm and peaceful voyage, Captain Smith's plan was gradually to increase the output from his new engines until—weather permitting—the *Titanic* achieved her top speed. On Sunday, 24 of the 29 boilers were lit, and it was expected that the others would be fired up imminently. Although J. Bruce Ismay would later strenuously deny that he had issued any instructions to Captain Smith to increase speed, he was certainly aware that this was Smith's intention; the general plan for performance testing had been agreed with all concerned prior to the commencement of the voyage. Charges would be leveled against Ismay that he had urged Smith to abandon caution and "go for the record" to win the Blue Riband on the *Titanic*'s first Atlantic crossing. This was patent nonsense, especially given Ismay's disdain of the race and the fact that he knew full well that the *Titanic* would never be capable of the matching *Mauretania*'s 26 knots.

On Sunday morning the *Titanic*'s Marconi operators picked up a message from the Cunard liner *Caronia*, which reported that icebergs, growlers (smaller icebergs) and field ice had been spotted just north of the *Titanic*'s intended route. Captain Smith made sure that all of his officers were aware of the report; they would all also have been aware that the tendency would be for

First Officer Murdoch, Chief Officer Wilde, Fifth Officer Lowe and Captain Smith on the deck of the *Titanic*.

this ice to drift south. A second ice warning was received from the Dutch liner *Noordam* later in the morning. In the early afternoon, yet another warning came in, this time from the White Star liner *Baltic*. The captain of the *Baltic* reported that a Greek steamer had tracked icebergs and field ice that day in very close proximity to the *Titanic*'s position. Captain Smith showed this message to Ismay, an act that would subsequently be used to sustain the argument that Ismay, not Captain Smith, was running the ship. The message was more likely to have been shown merely for Ismay's information, and Ismay certainly felt it of sufficient interest to show it to a number of other passengers before Captain Smith reclaimed it several hours later and had it posted on the bridge for the benefit of his officers.

Shortly after the message from the *Baltic*, the *Titanic* received yet another warning of icebergs in her vicinity, this time from the U.S. Navy's Hydrographic Department, broadcasting to all ships in the North Atlantic. For reasons unknown, this message was never passed from the radio room to Captain Smith. During the course of Sunday afternoon, the outside temperature dropped dramatically, and passengers were forced indoors for the warmth and comfort of the ship's lounges. As night began to fall and the light started to fade, lookouts were specifically instructed to watch for icebergs.

Lookouts without binoculars

The *Titanic* had six crewmen whose sole job was to scan the waters ahead of the ship for signs of trouble. They worked in two-man teams in the crow's nest, a small sheltered platform 50 ft. (15 m) up the forward mast. Their shifts lasted two hours, giving them a four-hour break between watches. Normally, given

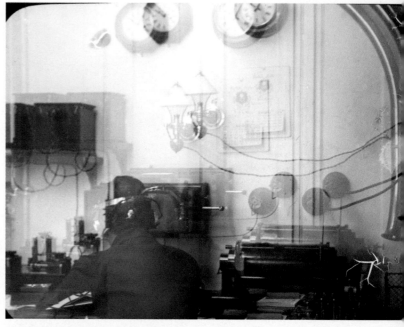

Above: One of Francis Browne's photographs of wireless operator Harold Bride on duty in the radio room listening for signals. Bride and Phillips received numerous Morse messages warning of ice in the *Titanic*'s path, but not all of them were brought to the captain's attention straightaway.

Below: The ice mountain that sealed the *Titanic*'s fate towered at least 75 feet above the surface of the sea, but it was the bulk of ice below the water that did the damage.

that officers on the bridge would also be watching where they were steering the ship, the two lookouts would have been perfectly adequate. But it was common practice on merchant vessels to post extra lookouts, particularly a forward lookout on the bow, when there was a likelihood of encountering ice. No such lookout was posted aboard the *Titanic*. However, First Officer Murdoch did order that the forecastle hatch should be closed to block light from below and that all forward lights should be extinguished to avoid them interfering with the sight lines from the bridge and the crow's nest.

In the crow's nest itself, the two lookouts were annoyed not to have been given binoculars, despite having asked for them in Southampton. Binoculars had been issued to lookouts on the journey from Belfast to Southampton, but none were available thereafter. No adaquate explanation has ever been given for not having issued binoculars to the lookouts. Second Officer Lightoller later admitted that there were several pairs on the

bridge. And when questioned at the subsequent inquiry, the lookout Frederick Fleet claimed that with binoculars he could certainly have seen the iceberg sooner; when asked how much sooner, he replied, "Enough to get out of the way."

By early evening, as the first of the passengers sat down to dinner in their respective dining rooms, the temperature plummeted to less than 40° F and a message was received from the Leyland Line freighter *Californian*—although it was actually intended for the cargo ship *Antillian*—advising of several large icebergs in the area. Captain Smith left a party being hosted in his honor by the Philadelphia banker George Widener, his wife, Eleanor, and their son, Harry, around 9:00 p.m. for a situation report from Second Officer Lightoller on the bridge. The temperature was now only a fraction above freezing, but it was decided that following common practice for shipping on this route at that time, they should maintain speed while keeping a sharp watch for ice. The

FIRST CLASS STATE ROOMS

POST MAIL ROOM

THE BUCKLED PLATES

BILGE KEEL

DOUBLE BOTTOM

KEEL

ICE PENETRATING THE DOUBLE BOTTOM

captain retired to his cabin at around 9:30 p.m.

Ten minutes later, while his subordinate Harold Bride was taking a break, Marconi operator Jack Phillips once again received an ice warning, this time from the Atlantic Transport Lines' *Mesaba*. Phillips, however, was attempting to clear the decks in preparation for his busiest period. Cape Race in Newfoundland was within transmission range, and Phillips was determined to deal with sending the backlog of messages from earlier in the day before passengers who had finished dinner chose to start bombarding him with more requests. Because of reduced interference at night, the Marconi set's range was vastly increased, so it was later in the evening when many passengers (only the wealthier ones, since a 10-word message cost 12s 6d–equivalent today to £150, almost U.S. $300) decided to telegraph friends and relatives to update them on news of the voyage. Having passed on so many ice warnings, Phillips decided to set this one aside–just as he had done with the warning from the U.S. Navy–for delivery to the bridge at a more convenient moment. If Phillips had given the message a higher priority, someone on the bridge might have considered it in conjunction with the other warnings–all of which gave

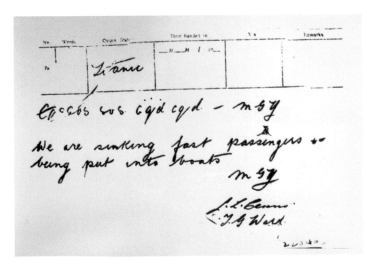

Above: Several ships picked up the *Titanic*'s distress calls, including the *Birma*, whose wireless operators took down this message sent by Jack Phillips, who was sending SOS calls, as well as the older CQD and the *Titanic*'s call sign MGY.

Opposite: This contemporary illustration shows how the plates buckled when the iceberg struck, although the apparent penetration of the ice into the hull is misleading.

positional coordinates for the ice sightings–and realized that the *Titanic* was heading straight into a maze of icebergs many miles wide, lying across her path like a frozen mountain range.

But such was the confidence of the *Titanic*'s officers in their "unsinkable" ship and the tried-and-true practice of trusting their lookouts that, even if Phillips had delivered the final warning, there is no guarantee that any further steps would have been taken. On such a clear night, they would surely have expected to spot anything lying in their path. When First Officer Murdoch relieved Second Officer Lightoller at 10:00 p.m., Lightoller told him that they could expect to see ice at any time. The temperature was now well below freezing, and Lightoller headed for his quarters and a warm bunk. He was not to rest for long.

The fatal collision

In the radio room, Phillips's work was interrupted by a signal from the *Californian* informing the *Titanic* that they were stopped and surrounded by ice, but Phillips cut the message short, telling the *Californian* operator not to jam his signal, as he was dealing with Cape Race. The operator desisted and listened in for a while longer before calling it a day. The *Californian* had no second operator to take over the monitoring of the radio, which was then effectively shut down for the night. Later, as the *Californian* waited for daylight amid the ice, her lookouts and duty officers would see rockets being fired from an unidentified ship–and would even attempt to make contact using their Morse lamp–but the ship's master, Stanley Lord, who had been woken from his sleep, remained unconvinced that the rockets signified anything sinister. Reluctant to try to maneuver his ship through the ice, Lord went back to sleep.

Cursing the cold high up in the *Titanic*'s crow's nest, the lookouts Reginald Lee and Frederick Fleet noticed a strange haze on the horizon. A few minutes later, at 11:40 p.m., Fleet spotted an iceberg at a distance later estimated to be no more than 500 yards (457 m) ahead. He immediately sounded three rings on the warning bell in the crow's nest and telephoned the bridge, informing Sixth Officer James Moody that an iceberg lay dead ahead. First Officer Murdoch ordered a turn to port to try to avoid the ice monster and instructed the engine room to give him full speed astern. He also flicked the switch to close the automatic watertight doors down in the bowels of the ship. He knew that with the *Titanic* traveling at over 22 knots, a collision was probably inevitable. Thirty seconds later, the great liner struck the iceberg.

The part of an iceberg that is visible above the surface of the water sits on a mass of ice around eight times bigger. The height of the visible part of the iceberg that Frederick Fleet had spotted looming out of the darkness was estimated at up to 100 ft. (30 m), but it was the massive submerged body of ice that did the damage. Having turned to port, the *Titanic* closed with the iceberg to starboard, and the glancing blow that she suffered was enough to slice a 300-ft. (90-m)-long incision into the hull below the waterline. The tear in the steel plates was not very wide, but it is likely that the impact also popped open some of the riveted joints between the plates. The collision did not cause any unduly worrying bump or crash. Some passengers heard a slight grinding noise, some felt a bit of a shudder, while others sleeping in their cabins noticed nothing at all. Even crew members working in the engine room didn't realize that the *Titanic* had struck something. In No. 6 boiler room, however, there was a boom like a clap of thunder, and water began pouring in through the slit in the ship's side. With the watertight doors closed, those who could scrambled up the ladder to the deck above to escape the rising torrent.

Captain Smith immediately realized that something was wrong and was on the bridge within a few seconds. Having been appraised of the situation and assured that the watertight doors were closed, he ordered Fourth Officer Boxhall below for a damage report. The other officers were alerted and hurried to the bridge, as did J. Bruce Ismay. Passengers who had lingered after dinner in the lounges chatting or playing cards ventured out on deck, and some saw the iceberg drifting away on the starboard side. Some even picked up chunks of ice from the deck as curiosities. No one thought for a moment that there was any danger of the ship sinking.

Down below on the Orlop Deck, First Officer Boxhall had a different picture. He saw the postal clerks rescuing mailbags from the water flooding into the mail storage room, attempting

SAVED BY "S.O.S.": "TITANIC" SURVIVORS IN THE LIFE-BOATS.

The first survivors of the *Titanic* were picked up in their lifeboats by the *Carpathia* just after 4:00 a.m. The Cunard liner, which had been heading eastward across the Atlantic, then spent five hours bringing survivors aboard and searching for more, before turning back for New York.

to manhandle them up to the post office on the deck above. He could also see that the water level was rising fast and reported back to Captain Smith. Accompanied by Thomas Andrews, Smith went below to see the damage for himself.

Andrews knew in an instant that the *Titanic* was doomed. She had been designed to stay afloat with two of her watertight compartments flooded. The iceberg had slashed open her   hull to let water into five compartments. Worse still, the bulkheads separating the compartments did not extend all the way up to the full height of the hull. As water filled the forward compartment, it would flood over the bulkhead into the second compartment, and from the second into the third, accelerating the rate at which the compartments flooded and the rate at which she settled at the bows. Andrews estimated that they had no more than two hours before the ship went down.

Ironically, had no evasive action been taken and had the

Titanic hit the iceberg head-on, the damage might have been confined to just one or two compartments, allowing her to stay afloat. Within ten minutes of the accident, there was over 10 ft. (3 m) of water in the first five compartments. Captain Smith now knew that he had no option but to order the evacuation of the ship. He also knew that he could provide only half of those on board with a space in a lifeboat.

Launching the lifeboats

There was some confusion among the crew when they were ordered to man the lifeboats. They had had little training with the new davits or their own specific tasks in the case of an emergency such as this. With no public-address system to let the passengers know what had happened, they, too, were somewhat confused. Crew members and stewards roused the first- and second-class passengers, helping them put on their lifejackets. When word spread to the third-class areas that the ship was sinking, many of the steerage passengers clogged the corridors trying to make their way up to the Boat Deck, all of their baggage in tow. Even when they were instructed to leave it behind, some persisted. For the wealthier passengers to leave behind all they were traveling with was one thing, but for many of the immigrants on their way to start a new life, losing their baggage meant losing everything they owned.

Meanwhile, Fourth Officer Boxhall was ordered to make a quick calculation of the *Titanic*'s position, and Captain Smith gave this to Phillips in the radio room so that he could send out a distress signal. Phillips, with Bride alongside him, sent out the international distress call CQD (often taken to mean "Come Quick Danger," although this is not strictly true), as well as the slightly more recent SOS, adopted because of its immediately recognizable Morse pattern and not, as is also often thought, to mean "Save Our Souls." Several ships and Cape Race picked up the *Titanic*'s distress call, but it was the Cunard liner *Carpathia* that emerged as the *Titanic*'s best hope of salvation, even though she was almost 60 miles (96 kilometers) away.

At 12:45 a.m. the first of the lifeboats was lowered. Captain Smith had ordered that women and children should go first, and the men (mainly first- and second-class passengers at this time)

helped the women climb into the lifeboats. Some of the women refused to leave their husbands, and many passengers preferred to stay with the mighty *Titanic* rather than take to the ocean in one of the flimsy-looking small boats, refusing to believe that the liner could actually sink. The first boat was lowered less than half full. Indeed, none of the boats were to leave the ship full. The crew were not confident that the boats could be safely lowered when full, and they were to take on more passengers from doors that were to be opened in the ship's side closer to the waterline. But the men who were sent to open those doors were never seen again, nor were the doors ever opened.

As the first boat was lowered, distress rockets were fired by Boxhall, who spotted a ship's lights about 6 miles (10 kilometers) away on the port side. Several other officers, including Captain Smith, also saw the lights, but the ship could not be contacted by radio or with the use of a Morse lamp. An hour after it was first sighted, it seemed to turn and disappear.

Courage amid the chaos

Among the confusion as the passengers and crew struggled to launch the lifeboats, there were scenes of desperate panic but also examples of calm, reserve and ultimate courage.

Colonel Astor saw his young wife, whom he knew to be pregnant, into a lifeboat; then promising to follow in the next available boat, he strode off calmly along the deck, lighting a cigarette. Madeleine was never to see her husband again.

Benjamin Guggenheim, who had been traveling with his valet, Victor Giglio, and chauffeur, Rene Perot, was seen watching the launching of the lifeboats then disappeared to his cabin with Giglio, the pair returning dressed in full evening attire. Guggenheim announced to all present that they had dressed up in their best and "were prepared to go down like gentlemen." None of the three survived.

Charles Joughlin, the ship's head baker, stayed to help passengers into the lifeboats as long as he was of use, even throwing children across the gap between the ship's side and the lifeboat to make sure that they escaped. He then went below to fortify himself with whiskey before the ordeal of being immersed in the icy Atlantic water. As he sought out a bottle, he

This page: When the news of the disaster broke, crowds of anxious relatives and friends besieged the White Star Line offices in London, Liverpool and on Broadway in New York, desperate for news of loved ones who had sailed on the *Titanic*.

Opposite: Wireless reports received from the *Carpathia* and other ships in the area were confused, with one report even suggesting that all of the *Titanic*'s passengers and crew had been saved, but the grim truth dawned when the *Carpathia* docked in New York.

met one of the ship's surgeons with similar intent. Joughlin survived the sinking and was picked up by a lifeboat. Neither of the *Titanic*'s surgeons was so lucky.

Shots are fired

Much has been made in movies about the sinking of the use of revolvers by the officers to maintain order. Purser McElroy was certainly reported to have fired a shot or shots into the air, and Second Officer Lightoller drew his weapon when ordering men to form a human barrier to hold back panicking male passengers to stop them from swamping the lifeboats. Fifth Officer Lowe also confirmed that he had discharged his weapon to deter third-class passengers from storming the lifeboats but reliable and unambiguous reports of officers having shot passengers or officers having committed suicide are difficult to pin down. There is little doubt that the scene in James Cameron's *Titanic* movie where First Officer Murdoch shoots himself is a fabrication. Some surviving passengers did claim to have seen an officer shoot himself, but their accounts tend to contradict one another, and the most reliable reports have Murdoch with Chief Officer Wilde frantically trying to release the last collapsible boat when they met their doom.

Many of the most notable of the high society figures aboard were drowned, including Colonel Astor, George and Harry Widener, Major Archie Butt, Arthur Ryerson, Isidor and Ida Straus, and Charles M. Hays—but the greatest death toll among the passengers was in third-class, with over 440 perishing. Although there were sufficient life belts for everyone on board, no one who was left floating in the water could hope to survive in the freezing temperature for very long. By the time the *Carpathia* arrived on the scene at around 4:00 a.m., only those lucky enough to have secured a lifeboat place were left alive. After spending some five hours bringing the survivors aboard and searching for more, the *Carpathia*, which had finally been joined by the *Californian*, left the scene, heading for New York.

The *Carpathia* arrived in New York at around 9:25 p.m. on April 18, 1912. A great crowd of anxious relatives and friends, as well as overeager press reporters, had gathered at the Cunard liner's usual berth. But the *Carpathia* headed instead for

the White Star Line pier, where she deposited the *Titanic*'s lifeboats before finally docking at the Cunard facility.

The United States Senate Inquiry into the sinking of the *Titanic* was launched with seemingly indecent haste at the Waldorf-Astoria hotel in New York on the morning of Friday, April 19. The inquiry was implemented at the instigation of the Michigan senator William A. Smith, a wealthy lawyer and newspaper proprietor. Senator Smith had sailed with Captain Smith previously and was determined to discover how a vessel with such an experienced master could come to grief. The number of prominent American citizens aboard the *Titanic* also generated massive interest in the tragedy, perpetuated by sensational headlines in the popular press.

The American inquiry

The day before the *Carpathia* docked in New York, as anxious relatives desperate for news of their loved ones formed crowds outside the White Star Line offices on Broadway, Senator Smith presented a resolution before the U.S. Senate in Washington, D.C., empowering the Committee of Commerce to hold an inquiry. Smith was appointed chairman of the sub-committee investigating the disaster. But when informed by the U.S. Navy that they had intercepted signals from J. Bruce Ismay stating that he would like to return directly to Britain with the *Titanic*'s crew without even setting foot on American soil, he hastily

Above left: One of the *Titanic*'s lifeboats pulls alongside the *Carpathia*. The photograph was heavily retouched at the time it was printed and an arrow was added, apparently pointing to J. Bruce Ismay.

Above right: Shocked survivors aboard the *Carpathia*, still scarcely able to believe the horrors they experienced.

convened the inquiry's first hearings. Senator Smith knew that subpoenas could not be served on foreign nationals compelling them to give evidence to the inquiry if they were not actually in the United States, and he wasn't about to let the man he wanted most—J. Bruce Ismay—slip through his fingers.

The hearings were to last 18 days, and the first witness to be called was J. Bruce Ismay. He arrived at the Waldorf-Astoria protected by bodyguards after having been portrayed as a despicable villain in the newspapers for escaping safely from his sinking ship while so many of his passengers drowned. He was accused of forcing Captain Smith to sail faster than was safe and of demanding a luxurious room aboard the *Carpathia* so as not to share the misery of the other survivors.

Ismay staunchly defended himself against these charges at the hearing both in New York and when the investigation was reconvened in Washington, D.C. He maintained that he had boarded the Englehardt collapsible boat "C" only when there were no women, children or other passengers around and that he was in such a state of distress when he was brought aboard

the *Carpathia* that he didn't know what was happening to him. He was actually given the ship's doctor's quarters.

Senator Smith interrogated Ismay intensely and at length on everything from technical aspects of the ship and the health of Captain Smith, to the speed of the vessel and the £70,000 per year received by the White Star Line from the British government for transporting the mail. While repeatedly assuring the inquest that he would cooperate fully with the inquiry, provide written affidavits or attend later hearings if required, Ismay submitted a written request for permission to return home on April 25, noting that the British Board of Trade was in the process of establishing its own inquiry into the disaster, which would require his presence. Smith dismissed his request, ordering Ismay to remain in the United States and warning him that "you should continue to help me instead of annoying me and delaying my work by your personal importunities."

Lifeboats for all on board

Ismay did state during the inquiry that as a result of the disaster, the watertight bulkheads on White Star Line ships would, in future, extend higher to avoid the problem of water flooding over and into the next compartment. He also stated that "we have issued orders that none of the ships of our lines shall leave any port carrying more passengers and crew than they have capacity for in the lifeboats."

The subcommittee's final report was mainly a matter-of-fact appraisal of events leading up to the disaster, the cause of the sinking and a review of those involved. It also recommended that the existing practice of accepting foreign certificates of seaworthiness as being of equivalent merit to the U.S. version be reviewed and that no ship carrying passengers be allowed to leave a U.S. port unless it conformed to U.S. standards. The committee further advised that U.S. standards should be reviewed to ensure that ships were required to have lifeboat places for every passenger and crew member, that ships' radios should be manned 24 hours a day and that the firing of rockets at sea, except as distress signals, should be made a criminal offense. The area where the report was most scathing was in the conduct of the *Californian* and Captain Lord. It stated that:

The committee was forced to the inevitable conclusion that the *Californian*, controlled by the same company, was nearer the *Titanic* than the 19 miles [30 kilometers] reported by her Captain, and that her officers and crew saw the distress signals of the *Titanic* and failed to respond to them....Had assistance been promptly proffered, or had the wireless operator of the *Californian* remained a few minutes longer at his post on Sunday evening, that ship might have had the proud distinction of rescuing the lives of the passengers and crew of the *Titanic*.

Captain Smith to blame

Senator Smith was far more colorful in the address he made to the Senate when presenting the report on what he described as "the causes leading up to the destruction of the steamship *Titanic*, with its attendant and unparalleled loss of life, so shocking to the people of the world." While he criticized Captain Lord just as heavily as the written report, he also scolded the British Board of Trade for its "laxity of regulation and hasty inspection." But Senator Smith laid the lion's share of the blame for the accident squarely at the door of Captain Smith. While praising the captain's good record and fine character, Smith lambasted him for displaying "overconfidence and neglect to heed the oft-repeated warnings of his friends," bluntly stating that "his indifference to danger was one of the direct contributing causes of this unnecessary tragedy."

The findings of the U.S. inquiry were reviewed by the press on both sides of the Atlantic. Although the official report was generally welcomed by all, Senator Smith's comments and the fact that he bombarded the witnesses with questions in what was seen as an unnecessarily aggressive manner, were roundly condemned. The British *Daily Express* wrote, "Although much of the report sounds sensible, the grotesque oration of Senator Smith deprives it of much value.... Its mock heroics and ludicrous verbosity relieve it of any taint of sincerity or sense."

The British inquiry into the tragedy was ordered by the Board of Trade and headed by Charles Bigham, Lord Mersey. The

J. Bruce Ismay faced some stiff questioning about his role in the disaster. But he defended himself staunchly both at the hastily convened Senate Inquiry in New York and at this hearing in Washington, D.C.

board drew up a list of 26 questions to which it required answers from the investigation. These questions ranged from establishing the number of people on board the ship, whether it was adequately designed, manned and equipped, and what precautions were taken when entering the area where ice warnings had been issued, to the details of the accident, the allocation of lifeboat places and the number and status of those saved. Special reference was made to the proportions of first-, second- and third-class passengers who had been saved to determine whether preferential treatment had been given to the more well-heeled passengers. The hearings were opened in the Wreck Commissioner's Court, Royal Scottish Drill Hall, Buckingham Gate, Westminster, on May 2, 1912. The first day was taken up with legal representations and establishing protocol. The first of the 97 witnesses to give evidence, the *Titanic* lookout Archie Jewell, was called on day 2.

Jewell was questioned about his recollections of the night of the disaster, setting the scene for the testimonies of those to follow. Among those, on days 11 and 12 of the hearings, was that of Sir Cosmo Duff Gordon. Duff Gordon had been heavily criticized for taking a place in Boat No. 1, which had been launched at around 1:10 a.m. and was by no means the last of the boats to leave, while there were still so many women on board. Accusations were leveled against him that he had bribed the seamen at the oars of the boat to row away from the area of the wreck after the *Titanic* had gone down. Even though the boat was capable of taking at least 40, only 12 people (including seven crew members) were aboard. They had, therefore, space to take on at least 28 survivors from the water but made no attempt to return for any.

Accusations of bribery

In his testimony to the inquiry, Leading Fireman Charles Hendrickson, one of the crew members ordered to man Boat No. 1, claimed that they had obeyed the orders they had been given when the boat was launched and had pulled away from the *Titanic* for 200 yards (182 m) before stopping to wait for further orders or to be recalled. When the ship went down, he claimed the cries of those in the water were clearly audible, yet when he suggested that they return to pick up survivors, Sir Cosmo and Lady Duff Gordon had objected because "they were scared to go back for fear of being swamped." It had been claimed that Duff Gordon had offered each of the seamen £5 to ignore the cries for help because the panicking passengers in the water would capsize the boat when too many of them tried to climb aboard.

Duff Gordon strenuously rebutted all of these accusations, maintaining that the money he had given to the men had been to help them replace their lost kit. He had been told during a conversation with one of the men in the boat that the White Star Line would stop their pay from the moment the ship sank and that they would receive no compensation for their loss. His gift of £5 to each man was made out of compassion and not as any sort of bribe. The money was duly handed over when the boat's occupants were picked up by the *Carpathia*. But whatever the circumstances surrounding the payment, the fact that Duff

Gordon had boarded a boat while other distinguished gentlemen had stayed behind and had not returned to rescue other survivors scarred him with a dishonor that would shame him for the rest of his days.

Following his experience at the hands of Senator Smith in America, J. Bruce Ismay took the stand in Westminster on days 16 and 17 of the British inquiry, well prepared for a repeat of his ordeals in New York and Washington, D.C. He faced the same sort of questions with which Senator Smith had confronted him and answered them in much the same fashion, fully aware that Lord Mersey's team had transcripts of all of the Senate Inquiry's witness statements to which they could refer. The Wreck Commissioner's Inquiry, however, seemed less intent on pinning the blame for the sinking of the *Titanic* on Ismay. When his report was finally published on July 30, 1912, Lord Mersey stated that there had been:

> ...the suggestion that, as Managing Director of the Steamship Company, some moral duty was imposed upon him to wait on board until the vessel foundered. I do not agree. Mr. Ismay, after rendering assistance to many passengers, found "C" collapsible, the last boat on the starboard side, actually being lowered. No other people were there at the time. There was room for him and he jumped in. Had he not jumped in he would merely have added one more life, namely his own, to the number of those lost.

Lord Mersey was less kind about Sir Cosmo Duff Gordon:

> I have said that the members of the crew in that boat might have made some attempt to save the people in the water, and that such an attempt would probably have been successful; but I do not believe that the men were deterred from making the attempt by any act of Sir Cosmo Duff Gordon's. At the same time I think that if he had encouraged the men to return to the position where the *Titanic* had foundered, they would probably have made an effort to do so and could have saved some lives.

Following the sinking of the *Titanic*, many alterations were made to the *Olympic* in light of the lessons learned from her sister ship's design flaws. The third of the *Olympic*-class liners, the *Gigantic*, incorporated the redesigned bulkhead and watertight compartment designs during her construction two years later. She was renamed the *Britannic* in an effort to break the link with the *Titanic*.

CHAPTER EIGHT

AFTERMATH

Having considered all of the evidence, the Wreck Commissioner's Inquiry found that the *Titanic* was lost "due to collision with an iceberg, brought about by the excessive speed at which the ship was being navigated." Just as the U.S. report had done, Lord Mersey laid most of the blame for the unnecessary loss of life during the disaster at the feet of Captain Lord and the crew of the *Californian*. The captain and the relevant members of his crew were questioned at length; ultimately Lord Mersey surmised that:

> The vessels were about five miles [eight kilometers] apart at the time of the disaster. The evidence from the *Titanic* corroborates this estimate, but I am advised that the distance was probably greater, though not more than eight to ten miles [twelve to sixteen kilometers]. The ice by which the *Californian* was surrounded was loose ice extending for a distance of not more than two or three miles [three or four kilometers] in the direction of the *Titanic*. The night was clear and the sea was smooth. When she first saw the rockets, the *Californian* could have pushed through the ice to the open water without any serious risk and so have come to the assistance of the *Titanic*. Had she done so, she might have saved many if not all of the lives that were lost.

Again in accordance with Senator Smith's findings, Lord Mersey recommended that ships should be built with watertight compartments that were divided longitudinally and extended up to the highest main deck. Such designs should be created in conjunction with a double bottom that extended above the waterline. He further recommended that the Board of Trade be given immediate powers to enforce such regulations. As far as lifeboats were concerned, Lord Mersey called for a lifeboat space for every person on board every ship and insisted that drills should be held more regularly.

He did not find that the third-class passengers had been deliberately neglected at the expense of those in first and second class, but he did criticize the procedure on the *Titanic* for manning the lifeboats. The report stated that there was no evidence to suggest that "the third-class passengers had been unfairly treated; that their access to the Boat Deck had been impeded, and that when at last they reached that deck, the first- and second-class passengers were given precedence in getting places in the boats."

Nevertheless, only 38 percent of the third-class passengers were saved, compared with more than 60 percent in first class and more than 40 percent second class. Lord Mersey stated that the greater proportion of first- and second-class passengers saved could be accounted for "by the greater reluctance of the third-class passengers to leave the ship, by their unwillingness to part with their baggage, by the difficulty in getting them up from their quarters, which were at the extreme ends of the ship, and by other similar causes."

British inquiry a whitewash

Lord Merseys assertions, along with the statement of Mr. Harbinson, who attended the inquiry to represent the interests of relatives of some of the third-class passengers who died, has led to the report being called a whitewash. Harbinson declared that "no evidence has been given in the course of this case which would substantiate a charge that any attempt was made to keep back the third-class passengers."

The whitewash accusations also extended to Lord Mersey's appraisal of the conduct of Captain Smith leading up to the disaster. Although the report stated quite clearly that the collision with the iceberg was "brought about by the excessive speed," Lord Mersey accepted, on the evidence given by captains of other ships, that "for a quarter of a century or more the practice of liners using this track when in the vicinity of ice at night had been in clear weather to keep the course, to maintain the speed and to trust to a sharp lookout to enable them to avoid the danger." This policy had not in the past resulted in any major accidents or loss of life, and Lord Mersey sympathized with Captain Smith, who "had not the experience which his own misfortune has afforded to those whom he has left behind." In Lord Mersey's opinion, having received warnings of ice but deciding not to slow the ship or post extra lookouts, Captain Smith had:

...made a mistake, a very grievous one, but one in which, in face of the practice and of past experience, negligence cannot be said to have had any part; and in the absence of negligence, it is, in my opinion, impossible to fix Captain Smith with blame. It is, however, to be hoped that the last has been heard of the practice and that for the future it will be abandoned for what we now know to be more prudent and wiser measures. What was a mistake in the case of the *Titanic* would without doubt be negligence in any similar case in the future.

Captain Smith was, therefore, exonerated by Lord Mersey. The same could not be said for Captain Lord. Following the controversy of the U.S. and British inquiries, he was forced to resign from the Leyland Line. He joined a London freight line, the Nitrate Producers Steam Ship Company, as a ship's captain, remaining with that company until he retired in 1927.

Lord fought to clear his name in the aftermath of the inquiries, insisting that the *Californian* was farther away and that she was not the ship seen by those on board the *Titanic*. He finally decided to try to put it all behind him, but each film released or book published about the disaster—where he was inevitably painted as the villain of the peace—caused him great distress.

When the 1958 movie *A Night to Remember* was released, Lord made one last attempt to salvage his good name, and it finally emerged that another vessel may have been in the area. A Norwegian vessel had been illegally hunting seals in Canada and had been heading home via the route where the *Titanic* struck the iceberg. The Norwegians had no radio and took the distress rockets to be a Canadian government vessel signaling them to stop. They didn't. Even if the Norwegian ship was the one seen by the *Titanic*, it doesn't excuse the *Californian* for having failed to act once the distress rockets were seen.

The man appointed by the British Board of Trade to lead the official Wreck Commissioner's Inquiry into the *Titanic* tragedy was Lord Mersey, seen here with his son. The British hearings opened in Westminster, London, on May 2, 1912.

Stanley Lord died in 1962, but the debate about the *Californian* raged on, especially when the wreck of the *Titanic* was discovered in September 1985 by a team from the Woods Hole Oceanographic Institute of Massachusetts—13 miles (21 kilometers) from the position given in her distress signals. The truth about the position of the *Californian* in relation to the *Titanic* on the night of April 14, 1912, may never be known.

The *Titanic*'s officers

Although the *Titanic*'s surviving officers—once seen as the cream of the White Star Line—were not castigated in the same way as Captain Lord, their careers never recovered from the association with the disaster. None of the four ranking officers was ever to be given command of his own vessel. Second Officer Charles Herbert Lightoller served with the Royal Navy during the World War, after which he became chief officer of the White Star Line's *Celtic*. When it became clear that his seafaring career stood little chance of progressing much further, he retired, not yet 50 years of age, with 30 years of experience at sea. He ran a chicken farm and kept a yacht called the *Sundowner*, which he sailed across the English Channel in 1940 as part of the makeshift evacuation fleet called upon to rescue Allied troops from the beaches of Dunkirk.

Third Officer Herbert John Pitman persevered with his naval career through both the First and Second World Wars, and was awarded an MBE in 1946 for his unstinting service to Britain's Merchant Navy. Fourth Officer Joseph Boxhall had two notable reunions with the *Titanic*, although the first was on Ruislip Reservoir. The reservoir, close to Pinewood Studios, was used to shoot some of the scenes during the making of the 1958 movie *A Night to Remember*, on which Boxhall was employed as a technical adviser. Joseph Boxhall's second encounter with the great ship was in 1967, when his ashes were scattered in the Atlantic over the spot where the *Titanic* came to grief.

Fifth Officer Harold Lowe, who had fired the warning shots to stop panicking third-class passengers from storming the lifeboats, became Third Officer on the White Star Line's *Medic*, one of the company's "Jubilee" class of ships providing regular service between Britain and Australia. At just 12,000 tons, the *Medic* was a fraction of the *Titanic*'s size, could accommodate only 320 passengers and made a mere 13.5 knots, although she could carry a substantial load of freight. No one, however, would have regarded Lowe's posting to the *Medic* as a promotion. During the First World War, Lowe served in the Royal Navy and afterwards decided to retire from the sea.

Ismay the hero

The men involved in the building of the *Titanic* emerged from the catastrophe faring far better than her surviving officers. J. Bruce Ismay returned home to Liverpool, where he was greeted as a hero; several women had testified to Lord Mersey's inquiry that they owed their lives to Ismay because he ushered them into lifeboats. Although he was vilified by the American press, a statement he gave to *The Times* and the support he received from Lord Mersey stood Ismay in good stead at home. Nevertheless, he was often said to be a "broken man" who had been forced into retirement just over a year after the sinking of the *Titanic*. In fact, Ismay had been planning his retirement from IMMC and the White Star Line for some time prior to the accident. He had numerous other business interests, which he maintained up until around 1920, when he sold "Sandheys." He then divided his time between his London home and a country house, Costelloe Lodge in County Galway, where he fished for salmon in the Casla River that flowed through the grounds. He was said to have caught over 300 salmon there in one season.

When Costelloe Lodge was destroyed by fire, Ismay oversaw the rebuilding program and continued to enjoy family holidays there with his wife, Florence, and their children and grandchildren. In 1936 circulatory disease forced the amputation of his right leg, and his health continued to deteriorate until he died of a stroke in October 1937 at the age of 74. Following the death of her husband, Florence Ismay, who had become a British subject after her marriage, spent many years visiting her children, grandchildren and relatives in England and America. In 1949 she took an Oath of Repatriation to become an American citizen once more, although she spent her final days in England, where she died in 1963.

One of the *Titanic*'s four surviving officers,
Third Officer Boxhall, was employed as a
technical adviser on the 1958 movie *A
Night to Remember*.

Morgan a broken man

J. Bruce Ismay's ultimate boss, J. P. Morgan, was in Europe when the *Titanic* was due to set sail for New York and was expected to return to the United States aboard the pride of IMMC's fleets. He had a suite booked—suite B52, supposedly designed to his own taste and the accommodation that would be reserved for him whenever he crossed the Atlantic. Morgan did not, however, join the ship for the journey because the 75-year-old tycoon claimed that he was too ill to travel. Suite B52 was occupied by Ismay, his valet, John Fry, and his secretary, William Harrison, both of whom were drowned. J. P. Morgan may well have felt too poorly to contemplate the transatlantic voyage, but two days after the *Titanic* sank, a newspaper reporter managed to track him down at the French health resort of Aix-les-Bains, where Morgan was staying at the spa town's Grand Hotel in the company of his French mistress.

J. P. Morgan had weathered many financial storms and economic disasters throughout his checkered career, but the *Titanic* tragedy was believed by some to have affected him deeply. Financially, the loss of the *Titanic* and the subsequent compensation claims were a huge, but not terminal, setback to his plans for a North Atlantic monopoly. The political situation in Europe as the continent slid inexorably toward war played a far bigger role in thwarting his schemes. In any case some of the monetary losses were covered by insurance.

The loss of prestige in the face of the competition, however, could never be fully recovered. But more even than that, the deaths of 1,500 passengers were said to have weighed heavily on the old man. Perhaps this was because he believed those passengers had trusted him, through his shipping conglomerate, to carry them safely across the ocean and J. P. Morgan was a man who placed a great deal of value in trust. He

once told a U.S. congressional committee that capital and assets were not what mattered most to him as a banker when considering offering credit. The thing that mattered most was the character of the applicant: "A man I do not trust could not get money from me on all the bonds in Christendom." J. P. Morgan died at age 76, a year after the sinking of the *Titanic*.

Lord Pirrie goes to war

Another VIP who was scheduled to sail on the *Titanic*'s first Atlantic crossing, and also canceled because of illness, was one of the masterminds behind the building of the ship–Lord Pirrie. Following the sinking of the *Titanic*, he remained in charge at Harland & Wolff when the *Olympic* returned to the yard to have her bulkheads modified, her double bottom extended and to be equipped with new lifeboats. Politically, Pirrie had a rough ride in Belfast in 1912 because of his

Far left: Two years after the sinking of the *Titanic*, the First World War broke out and the Harland & Wolff yard was busier than ever. Here the light cruiser *Vindictive* is launched from *Olympic*'s No. 2 slipway.

Left: Harland & Wolff's shipbuilding program during the Second World War made them a prime target for Germany's Luftwaffe, and in May 1941 almost half of the yard was destroyed in bombing raids.

support for Home Rule, but on the business front, Harland & Wolff went from strength to strength under his guidance. They bought another shipyard at Govan on the Clyde, and when the First World War broke out in 1914, Pirrie's energy and talents in shipbuilding were utilized to the full in service of his country.

He was happy to be called upon to devote all of Harland & Wolff's resources to helping the war effort. He oversaw the conversion of 14 merchant ships into armed cruisers before launching into a massive warship-construction program. Ten gunships were built before the company began work on the light cruisers *Glorious* and *Vindictive*, which were modified during construction to carry aircraft. Lord Pirrie even established an aircraft manufacturing plant, where Harland & Wolff constructed the Avro 504 fighter bomber. He was made Comptroller-General of Merchant Shipping and laid out a whole new yard to mass-produce "standard" ships of identical design quickly and cheaply to replace vessels lost during the conflict. In 1917 Harland & Wolff built five "standard" ships and within a year had built 11 more, with 23 more on order.

In 1921 Lord Pirrie became a viscount and in 1922 was one of the first senators elected to the new parliament in Northern Ireland. He was also made a Knight of St. Patrick, a member of the Privy Councils of both Ireland and England, Chancellor of Belfast's Queen's University and High Sheriff of County Antrim and County Down. In 1924 Viscount Pirrie, accompanied by the viscountess, embarked on a tour of ports in Brazil, Uruguay, Argentina, Chile, Peru and Ecuador to study shipping prospects for the Pacific Steam Navigation Company, of which he was a stockholder. On his way to New York on the PSNC's liner *Ebro*, the 77-year-old viscount died of bronchial pneumonia.

Viscount Pirrie's brother-in-law, Alexander Carlisle, did not sail on the liner he had played such a prominent part in creating, but this was not entirely through his own choice. He traveled from his London home to Southampton to watch the *Titanic*'s departure and was purportedly asked why he was not on board; he replied that he had not been invited. Carlisle was married with three children, and after his retirement from Harland & Wolff, he became something of an eccentric figure, collecting autographs and riding a bicycle around London before it had become even remotely fashionable. He also swam every day, whatever the weather, in the Serpentine in Hyde Park. A year after the death of his brother-in-law, Alexander Carlisle, age 71, died after catching a severe chill.

Harland & Wolff faces the future

The company to which both men had devoted so much of their lives and whose workforce produced the *Titanic* grew ever more powerful as the years progressed. The Musgrave Yard founded by Lord Pirrie became the focus of Harland & Wolff's output, playing as vital a role in the company's efforts during the Second World War as it had during the First World War.

Over the 30 years or so that encompassed the two wars and the interwar period, Harland & Wolff produced almost 140 ships for the British Navy, including six aircraft carriers. One of the ships was the cruiser HMS *Belfast*, named after the city in which she was built. HMS *Belfast* was launched on St. Patrick's Day, March 17, 1938, and commissioned into the Royal Navy just one month before the Second World War began in 1939. She was soon in action but struck a mine while leaving the Firth of Forth in November 1939 and spent three years under repair. When she reentered the war, the *Belfast* was one of the most powerful ships in the Royal Navy. She escorted Arctic convoys and had the honor of firing some of the first shots during the bombardments in support of the D-Day landings. She now spends her retirement as a floating museum on the Thames in the shadow of Tower Bridge.

During that same 30-year period, Harland & Wolff also built around 130 merchant vessels, and their prolific output became a source of great irritation to the Germans. The Luftwaffe bombed the yards in April and May 1941, destroying over half of the facilities, but within two years Harland & Wolff was back to full production. After the Second World War, the Belfast shipyard continued to build some of the largest, most advanced ships in the world, including the aircraft carrier HMS *Eagle* and, in 1960, the luxury liner *Canberra*, the largest passenger ship to be built since the end of the war. *Canberra* herself saw military service when she carried troops to the Falklands in 1982.

Constantly evolving in order to stay at the forefront of the

shipbuilding industry, Harland & Wolff reorganized the Musgrave Yard in the early 1960s—doing much as Lord Pirrie had done over half a century before when preparing to build the Olympic-class liners—and converted six slipways into five larger ones to build ever bigger ships. They built Britain's first supertanker, the 190,000 ton *Myrina*, in 1969 and later developed a new process—prefabricating whole sections of a ship to be joined together rather than building the hull plate by plate.

Although the company continued to demonstrate its technical prowess, building highly advanced ships for the oil industry throughout the 1970s, '80s and '90s, Harland & Wolff became a symbol of Britain's industrial decay. It lost out on much needed shipbuilding orders to foreign competition to such an extent that by 1975 it was facing bankruptcy. Appalled at the prospect of thousands of Belfast workers losing their jobs, the British Government nationalized the yard, spending billions in subsidies trying to keep the business afloat. After almost 15 years of gradual decline, Harland & Wolff was bought back from the government by its own management and employees in partnership with the Norwegian shipping tycoon Fred Olsen. Sadly, it became impossible to maintain the company as a shipbuilder. The last ship to be constructed at Harland & Wolff was the ferry *Anvil Point* in 2003—on completion of which all but 130 of the workforce was made redundant.

The Belfast yard had at one time employed around 35,000 people. Harland & Wolff still exists, with regular contracts for the repair and maintenance of all kinds of vessels, as well as providing a design and technical consultancy to shipbuilders and the oil industry. They have even built bridges, ironic since they once employed a bridge builder to produce the gantry cranes required for the construction of the *Titanic* and *Olympic*.

Titanic's sister ship

RMS *Olympic* was soon back in service on the transatlantic run with her modifications and extra lifeboats in place. She continued to cross the Atlantic even after the First World War broke out, but the passenger trade dropped off when the U-boat menace made people realize that traveling thousands of miles in such a tempting target might not be such a good idea.

In 1915, when the *Olympic* was commissioned into the Royal Navy as HMT (His Majesty's Transport) *Olympic* to ferry service personnel to and from the Aegean, she was given a bizarre "dazzle" camouflage paint scheme. This was intended to break up her outline, making it harder for German submarine crews, to identify her through their periscopes and hopefully harder for them to fix an accurate range before launching their torpedoes.

In October 1914, the *Olympic* was ordered back to Belfast, where, once she had disembarked her passengers at Southampton, the White Star Line intended to mothball her until the war was over. On her way to Southampton, the *Olympic* rescued the entire crew of HMS *Audacious,* which had been crippled by a German mine, and took the warship in tow, although the tow lines parted in heavy seas and the *Audacious* had to be abandoned, her magazines later exploding and sealing her fate. Only six months later, *Olympic* was commissioned into the Royal Navy as a troop transport, and HMT (His Majesty's Transport) *Olympic* sailed for Greece resplendent in a bizarre multicolored camouflage scheme. The bold stripes and geometric shapes were intended to confuse enemy range-finders but had the effect of making the once graceful *Olympic* look like a graffiti victim.

With much of her luxurious interior stripped bare, the *Olympic* could carry up to 7,000 troops and was armed, following a further visit to Belfast in 1917, with antisubmarine guns. In 1918 the *Olympic* actually accounted for a German submarine, which she first shelled and then rammed, sinking it almost instantly—the only victory for any merchant ship against any German warship during the entire course of the war. The American servicemen the *Olympic* was carrying at the time donated money from an impromptu collection to have a plaque made for display aboard the *Olympic* in honor of this achievement. The *Olympic* ended the war carrying Canadian troops home before returning to Harland & Wolff to be refitted for regular passenger service. While she was being examined in Belfast, workers discovered a large dent in the *Olympic*'s hull, thought to have been caused by a German torpedo that, unknown to anyone, had struck the ship but failed to explode.

With her luxurious interior refitted and refurbished, the *Olympic* returned to cross the Atlantic under the flag of the White Star Line, having been converted to burn oil instead of coal. She suffered one desperately unfortunate incident in May 1934 when, approaching New York in heavy fog, the *Olympic* rammed and sank the Nantucket lightship. Seven of the lightship's crew were killed in the incident. The following year the *Olympic* was retired and, with no prospect of finding a buyer who might be willing to operate the aging liner as a working vessel, she was sold for scrap. The *Olympic*'s final voyage under her own steam was to Jarrow on the River Tyne, where she was stripped bare before her hull was towed to Inverkeithing on the Firth of Forth to be dismantled.

On Tyneside, her fittings were auctioned off. Much of her interior was bought by Douglas Smith, a director of the Smith and Walton paint factory, for £800. Smith and Walton's office complex was subsequently decorated with arched window frames from the *Olympic*'s gymnasium. The stateroom doors were used throughout the building, which also incorporated corridors of carved oak paneling from the main second-class staircase and the carved wooden entrance and doors to the second-class dining room. Smith and Walton's employees enjoyed eating in a canteen fitted with carved wood from the *Olympic*'s first-class smoking room, illuminated by lights from first-class passageways. Even the canteen toilets came from the *Olympic*.

The second sister

The company intended to build three *Olympic*-class sister ships and work began on the third ship—the *Gigantic*—on November 30, 1911. Her keel was laid on Slipway No. 1, where the *Olympic*'s construction had begun. When the *Titanic* was sunk five months later, work on the new ship was halted. In the light of the findings of both the U.S. and U.K. inquiries, as well as Harland & Wolff's and the White Star Line's own consideration of the causes of the disaster, it was clear that a major redesign was required. The epic name, intended to be the most inspiring of the trio—*Olympic*, *Titanic* and *Gigantic*—was also changed to the less imposing *Britannic*.

The work on new bulkheads and a double skin, along with other improvements, made the *Britannic* the largest of the three sister ships, at almost 50,000 tons. She had new lifeboat davits capable of handling six boats, although not all of the davits were of the new type when the *Britannic* left the yard in a hurry in December 1915. In February 1914, the *Britannic* was expected to enter transatlantic service in early 1915. But the outbreak of the First World War in the summer of 1914 put paid, not only to the plans for the *Britannic*'s maiden voyage but also her completion. Workers and materials were required for the war effort, and the luxury liner had to take second place.

Eventually the *Britannic* was called up for duty as a hospital ship, her interiors finished with hospital bunks and treatment rooms rather than opulent suites, smoking rooms, libraries and dining salons. She was painted white with a green stripe along her hull and red crosses to let the enemy know that this was a noncombatant ship. The *Britannic* left Belfast for Liverpool. Then, just before Christmas 1915, after embarking her crew and medical staff, she set out on her maiden voyage heading to the Greek island of Lemnos via Naples. On Lemnos, HMHS (His Majesty's Hospital Ship) *Britannic* took on casualties from the battles in the Dardanelles and headed for Southampton, where she docked in January 1916. Within a fortnight, she was headed back to Naples, where her orders were to bring casualties from other, smaller hospital ships back to the United Kingdom. After another similar trip, the *Britannic* spent a couple of months idle before being released by the Admiralty in June

1916. The *Britannic* headed back to Belfast to be completed to the White Star Line's requirements, but within two months the small port of Mudros on Lemnos was again a casualty clearing station and the *Britannic* was pressed into service once more.

The *Britannic*'s shuttle service between Southampton and the Aegean continued until November 21, 1916, when, having left Naples at around 8:00 a.m., a massive explosion on the starboard bow erupted as she negotiated the Kea Channel. It is unclear whether she struck a mine or was torpedoed. It has been speculated that the Germans believed the medical supplies she was carrying were actually munitions, and that made her a legitimate target. Thirty people died needlessly when the lifeboats they were in were lowered while the ship was still moving and the boats were sucked into the propellers, there to be smashed to pieces. The remainder of the passengers and crew escaped in lifeboats (the *Britannic* had 58) once the ship had been brought to a halt. The *Britannic* then sank 400 ft. (122 m) to the seabed—a shallow grave for such a grand ship. When her bow touched the bottom, her stern would still have been well above the surface.

Lusitania and Mauretania

The two ships that most inspired the building of the *Titanic*—the *Lusitania* and *Mauretania*—suffered fates strangely similar to their White Star rivals, the *Titanic* and *Olympic*. Like the *Olympic*, the *Mauretania* was requisitioned by the Admiralty for use as a troop transport during the First World War. Also like the *Olympic*, she was painted in a checkerboard of dazzle camouflage and sailed to the same ports as the *Britannic*, delivering and evacuating troops from Gallipoli and the Dardanelles campaign. In May 1919, she was released from wartime service and returned to England to be refitted as a luxury liner, but the refit did not include a complete overhaul of her turbines. Consequently, the *Mauretania*'s Atlantic crossing speeds were greatly reduced, since wartime service had left her engines badly in need of a major overhaul.

In July 1921, by which time the *Mauretania* was struggling to achieve 20 knots, a fire broke out, destroying much of the first-class accommodation and first-class dining room. The ship

During the First World War, Lord Pirrie established an aircraft manufacturing plant at Harland & Wolff, where the company produced the Avro 504 fighter bomber.

returned to the Tyneside yard of Swan, Hunter and Wigham Richardson, where she had been built, to undergo repairs. At the same time, her turbines were overhauled and the boilers converted to burn oil rather than coal. The six-month repair program included extensive modernization of the furnishing and fittings, and when she returned to service in March 1922, she was once again among the fastest and most luxurious passenger liners in the world. She achieved over 27 knots on one trip and broke her own record for the Atlantic crossing in both directions, but she was not quite fast enough to compete with the new German liner *Bremen*, which could make almost 29 knots and claimed the Blue Riband in 1929. The *Mauretania* made her last Atlantic crossing in September 1934. Stripped of her luxury furnishings, in July 1935 she made her final journey from Southampton to the breakers' yard at Rosyth, where, again like the *Olympic*, the aging liner ended her life.

The *Lusitania*'s career was, sadly, rather more like that of the *Titanic* in the way that it ended. She continued to operate as a passenger ship on the Atlantic route following the outbreak of the First World War until, on May 7, 1915, she was torpedoed by a German submarine off the southern coast of Ireland. The explosion was said to have sounded like a gigantic rumble of thunder and was followed shortly afterwards by a second blast— the source of which has become a point of great contention. This second explosion may have been caused by cold sea- water rushing in and engulfing the boilers, which would then have exploded, or it may have been a second torpedo.

One other explanation is that, as well as carrying civilian passengers, the *Lusitania* had in her holds a consignment of artillery shells and millions of rounds of small arms ammunition disguised as boxes of cheese and other regular cargo. Supplying such military aid to Britain in wartime would have contravened the laws of the then neutral United States and made the liner a perfectly legitimate target for the Germans. Whatever caused the second explosion, the *Lusitania* was doomed. Although 764 were rescued, 1,200 passengers—many of them American citizens—lost their lives in the tragedy and the outrage caused by the attack hastened America's entry into the First World War.

The White Star Line

Although the loss of the *Titanic* might have been expected to cripple the White Star Line, the company remained in strong competition on the Atlantic route despite the compensation claims and the publicity attracted by the huge sums involved. White Star paid out almost £3.5 million in compensation for the loss of life and property on the *Titanic*. The highest payment was made to Charlotte Drake Cardeza, whose list of lost belongings extended to over a dozen pages and amounted to £36,567, at the time well over $100,000. Despite all of this, White Star claimed a respectable percentage of the 2.6 million passengers who crossed the Atlantic in 1913. They carried over 191,000 passengers, which compared favorably with Cunard's total of almost 200,000. The German company Hapag, however, easily trumped this, with almost 250,000 passengers—the tide of U.S. immigrants continuing to flow most strongly from Germany and eastern Europe.

That was all to change the following year with the outbreak of war. From 1914 to 1918, much of the White Star fleet was either on military service or laid up for the duration of the war. The lack of passengers made maintaining a regular viable transatlantic service extremely difficult. Added to this was a shortage of coal (because of the navy's increased consumtion) and a lack of firemen, trimmers and other crew to man the ship after so many men were called up for military service. White Star managed to keep their passenger service running throughout the war years, except in 1917, but with a greatly reduced number of journeys.

After the war, business picked up and White Star was once again the jewel in IMMC's crown—for a while. In the 1920s, a depression in Europe and the economic insecurity of all but the richest Americans severely affected the North Atlantic passenger trade. There were fewer immigrants, fewer wealthy tourists heading for Europe and new U.S. legislation designed to protect its merchant fleets. As White Star Line ships sailed under the British flag, the company was seen by the IMMC as something of a liability. In 1927 it was sold off to become part of the Royal Mail Steam Packet Company (RMSPC).

Worse was to come. When the RMSPC began suffering in a

hostile economic climate, in 1934 the British government stepped in to offer a financial package that involved White Star merging with its old rival, Cunard. Construction of the *Queen Mary* was already under way for Cunard, and plans were well advanced for the building of the *Queen Elizabeth*. So when the merger went through, with Cunard the senior partner in the new Cunard–White Star Line, the building of White Star's *Oceanic III*–again intended to become the biggest ship in the world– was canceled. Both Cunard and White Star Line flags were flown on the new company's ships until the late 1950s, when Cunard took over completely. In 1960, the *Britannic* (the third White Star liner to bear the name) was scrapped, and the White Star Line was no more.

Cunard changes tack

Cunard continued to operate a transatlantic service, although the nature of the business changed completely. In the years following the Second World War, passenger traffic across the Atlantic was increasingly carried by aircraft, especially with the arrival of the jet age. Cunard's liners such as the *Queen Mary* (today a permanently docked hotel and shopping center in Long Beach, California) and the *Queen Elizabeth* (destroyed by fire while being converted to a floating university in Hong Kong in 1972) provided a pleasure-cruise alternative to air travel.

Then came the *Queen Elizabeth II*. While the *QE II* still crosses the Atlantic, she can just as readily be found during the winter months in sunnier climes, where her passengers embark on holiday cruises. This is a far more relaxed way to enjoy a luxury liner than in the days when such ships were forging across the Atlantic trying to set the fastest time for the crossing. Cunard's newest liner, the *Queen Mary II*, is the largest cruise ship in the world–as big as a modern aircraft carrier–entirely devoted to the comfort and entertainment of her passengers.

The *Titanic*, too, was intended to pander to the comfort and entertainment of her passengers, but unlike the *Queen Mary II*, her primary role was as part of a transatlantic shuttle service. The *Titanic* was expected to make money as part of an essential transport link rather than as a floating pleasure palace. The days of transatlantic steamship travel have all but gone. The purpose of the great liners has been reduced to that of a mobile holiday resort, but the modern world's last tenuous link with the *Titanic* has not yet completely dissolved. The White Star Line has gone, the North Atlantic passenger trade has gone, the original purpose of the great liners has gone, but one last link remains.

Titanic's tenders

Built for the specific task of servicing the Olympic-class liners at Cherbourg, the White Star Line tenders *Nomadic* and *Traffic* had working lives that far outstripped those of their parent ships. The *Traffic*, launched two days after the *Nomadic* at Harland & Wolff, was the one earmarked for ferrying third-class passengers from ship to shore as well as transferring baggage and mail sacks. She attended the *Titanic* just once, of course, but went on to serve a useful purpose in the First World War, ferrying troops from their mighty transport ships into Cherbourg, from where they would depart for the trenches far to the east.

She continued her civilian duties after the war until her role changed when she was sold to the Société Cherbourgeoise de Transbordment in 1927, after which she serviced any vessel in the port rather than working exclusively for the White Star Line. She was renamed the *Ingénieur Riebell* when the Société was reorganized in 1934. In 1940, as France was being overrun by the Germans during the Second World War, she was scuttled by the French navy. This effort was intended both to sabotage the port of Cherbourg and to make her useless to the enemy. The Germans, however, raised the *Ingénieur Riebell* and set her to work as an armed convoy escort. In January 1941, she was torpedoed and sunk while serving the Kriegsmarine.

Maintaining the link with the *Titanic*, therefore, is now the sole responsibility of the *Traffic's* sister ship, the *Nomadic*. Like the *Traffic*, the *Nomadic* ferried troops during the First World War and she was sold along with the *Traffic* in 1927, although a condition of the deal was that she should always be made available when required by White Star Line ships at Cherbourg. She became the *Ingénieur Minard* when the *Traffic* was renamed in 1934, and was involved in the evacuation of Allied troops from France in 1940. After the war, improvements to the harbor at Cherbourg and the decline in the transatlantic passenger trade meant that the *Ingénieur Minard* became increasingly redundant. The last grand liner she served was the *Queen Elizabeth* just before she retired to the Far East in 1968. The *Ingénieur Minard* was then sold off and left languishing by her new owner before she again changed hands and had her former name, the *Nomadic*, restored to her in 1974.

That last physical link with the *Titanic* may be in danger of crumbling away, but there is little chance that *Titanic* herself will ever be forgotten. There is, in fact, as much interest in the vessel around the world today as there ever has been.

She was taken to Paris, having been fitted out as a floating restaurant, and moored on the Seine near the Eiffel Tower for a number of years but again fell into disrepair. She was finally removed to Le Havre to await a fate that is as yet undecided. The neglected hulk of the *Nomadic*, a ship that took shape alongside the Olympic-class liners at Harland & Wolff, remains the last floating link with the building of the *Titanic*.

Titanic the movie star

The 1996 movie *Titanic*, starring Leonardo DiCaprio and Kate Winslet, used state-of-the-art computer-generated special effects as well as good old-fashioned water tanks and a 775-foot-long replica of the great liner. The replica, a temporary construction, was "sunk" so many times during filming that it eventually started falling apart. The movie became the most expensive film ever made, at $200 million, but earned its investors more money than any other movie, too—over $1,800 million! This was, of course, only the latest in the list of *Titanic* movies, which include *Raise the Titanic* in 1977, *The Unsinkable Molly Brown* (based on the story of the *Titanic* survivor Molly Brown) in 1960, *A Night to Remember* in 1958, *Titanic* in 1953, a German propaganda film called *Titanic* in 1943 and the very first movie, *Saved from the Titanic*, a silent film released in May 1912, just one month after the disaster. That first movie was cowritten by and starred actress Dorothy

The dawning of the jet age cut the time for an Atlantic crossing to a matter of hours rather than days, and the era of the ocean liner as an essential means of transport was over. Modern passenger liners like Cunard's *Queen Mary II* are now devoted to leisure and pleasure cruises rather than being the most vital link between America and Europe.

Gibson, who had been a passenger aboard the *Titanic* and was a survivor of the sinking. The *Titanic* has also starred or featured in countless TV shows and has been the subject of thousands of books. The whole world watched in wonder in 1985 when video footage of the newly discovered wreck, 13,000 feet down on the floor of the Atlantic, was released by Dr. Robert Ballard's survey team. There are successful, and highly professionally run, *Titanic* historical societies around the world, backed up by numerous Web sites, all dedicated to the preservation of information, photographs and artefacts from the ship. *Titanic* memorabilia, models, illustrations and images are big business.

The legend endures

Why is there such a continuing fascination with a ship that was built, and sank, over a century ago? There are a number of different ways to answer that question. Undoubtedly, the age-old motive of avarice has a part to play. Many believe that there are untold riches in jewels, gold and artefacts to be salvaged from the wreck, with various grandiose schemes proposed over the years to raise *Titanic*. It is highly unlikely that the remains of the *Titanic* will ever be moved from the bottom of the Atlantic. There have, however, been multiple attempts to plunder her treasure, although the wreck is now monitored in an attempt to preserve it as a memorial in the same way that sunken warships are protected as war graves.

The idea of treasure under the sea is enough to sustain a certain amount of interest on its own, but there are other sunken vessels that went down carrying valuable cargoes scattered far and wide over the ocean bed. So why does *Titanic* attract so much more attention than any other wreck? Certainly, this has a lot to do with what are often seen as the "unanswered" questions surrounding the disaster—why the ice warnings were ignored; why there appeared to be every intention of increasing rather than decreasing speed; why more first-class passengers were saved than third-class; why the *Californian* failed to respond to the distress rockets; why there were not enough lifeboats, or why neither Lord Pirrie nor J. P. Morgan joined the ship for her first Atlantic crossing. For some people, the obvious answers regarding standard practices,

arrogance, disorganization, confusion, possible negligence and the poor health of two elderly gentlemen simply will not suffice. If there is the merest hint of a blossoming mystery, then it must be plucked, savored and preserved. This has led to bizarre conspiracy theories involving the identities of the *Titanic* and the *Olympic* being switched based on the premise that the *Olympic*'s accidents had left her so badly damaged she was a "write-off." On her final repair trip to Belfast, so the theory goes, she was swapped for the new and pristine *Titanic*. The *Titanic*, disguised as the *Olympic*, then resumed service, while the *Olympic* was patched up to be sunk deliberately as the "Titanic" on her maiden voyage so that the owners could make a massive insurance claim. It is nonsense, but the theory has its devotees.

The real reason why the story of the *Titanic* has endured for almost a century is because of the people involved. The people who built the *Titanic*, the Belfast workers and their families, Lord Pirrie, J. Bruce Ismay, J. P. Morgan and everyone involved with the ship made sure that the whole world knew that this was the biggest, most modern, most remarkable vessel ever to put to sea. She was hailed as the ultimate luxury liner and regarded as "unsinkable," so her sinking naturally created a sensation. Among the passengers who died were some of America's wealthiest socialites, people whose names appeared regularly in the newspapers. Above all else, of course, was the terrible death toll. For 1,500 people to lose their lives in the accidental sinking of a ship in peacetime is a tragedy of immense proportions. Had the *Titanic* sunk with no casualties, everyone having escaped into lifeboats, none of the books, TV specials and movies devoted to the disaster would exist. Ask anyone what happened to the *Titanic*, where so many died, and they will probably be able to tell you about the ship that struck an iceberg. Ask them about what happened to the *Britannic*, where so many survived, and they won't have a clue.

The treasures that may be on board and the intrigue surrounding the disaster would be enough to sustain a certain level of interest in the ship, but the tales of heroism, forlorn hope and heartache surrounding those who perished and those who survived will ensure that the story of the *Titanic* endures for generations to come.

INDEX

2/06

DATE DUE

APR 21 '06			
MAY 16 '06			
MAY 23 '08			
NOV 6 '09			
JUN 17 '10			
MAY 10 '12			
OCT 31 '12			
FEB 04 2017			
FE 04 '17			
SEP 21 2017			

Demco, Inc. 38-293

Fig. 6 UPPER DECK (E)